FLORENCE NIGHTINGALE

by the same author

A GENERAL HISTORY OF NURSING

Florence Nightingale
by Lady Eastlake

FLORENCE NIGHTINGALE

LUCY RIDGELY SEYMER

FABER & FABER LIMITED
24 Russell Square
London

First published in mcml
by Faber and Faber Limited
24 Russell Square London W.C.1
Second impression mcmli
Third impression mcmliii
Printed in Great Britain by
Latimer Trend & Co Ltd Plymouth

Acknowledgments

I should like to tender my grateful thanks to the following: to Messrs. Harrison and Sons and Claud Morris (Books) Ltd. for permission to include the chapter 'Minding Baby'; to Messrs. Cassell for permission to reproduce the drawing of Embley Park; to Mr. Mitchelhill who provided me with the picture of Lea Hurst, and to Mrs. Vaughan Nash who allowed me to reproduce the Frontispiece. I am also greatly indebted to Miss V. Truman and Miss D. Rowe who read the typescript and made many helpful criticisms and suggestions. My husband very kindly drew the map on p. 41, and also gave me much valuable advice. Finally, Dr. May Thorne courteously furnished me with personal recollections of Florence Nightingale.

L. R. S.

Contents

Introduction   *page* xiii
1. Childhood and Youth   1
2. Aspirations and Training. The Institute of
   Deaconesses at Kaiserswerth and the Establishment for Gentlewomen   15
3. The Outbreak of the Crimean War   38
4. The Close of the Crimean War   65
5. War's Aftermath. Florence Nightingale's Work
   for the Royal Commissions   74
6. The Founding of the Nightingale School and
   Florence Nightingale's Other Work for
   Nursing   88
7. Florence Nightingale's Work for India   106
8. Her Other Interests and Some of Her Friends   114
9. Florence Nightingale's Writings   121
10. The Last Years   134
    Appendices   139
    Index   151

Illustrations

PLATES

Florence Nightingale, By Lady Eastlake   *frontispiece*
1. Embley Park, from a sketch by Parthenope
     Nightingale   *facing page* 2
2. Lea Hurst   2
3. Florence Nightingale and her nurses at Scutari   66
4. Florence Nightingale in the hospital at Scutari   66
5. Florence Nightingale in 1906   82

IN THE TEXT

1. Florence Nightingale's Diary, 1828   *page* 6
2. Map illustrating the Crimean Campaign   41
3. Florence Nightingale's handwriting, 1879   122

Introduction

Florence Nightingale's long life covered five reigns and forms a link between late Georgian and modern times. When she was born in 1820 England was mainly an agricultural country with few large towns and no railways. There were also no motors, no electric lights, no telephones, no aeroplanes. When she died in 1910 England was covered with cities and railways, cars could be seen on every road, electric lights and telephones were in common use and the future possibilities of aviation had been shown by Blériot when he flew the Channel in 1909. These external changes were matched by others quite as great in the way people lived and the opinions they held. But perhaps the greatest difference of all between 1820 and 1910—in any case the difference which is most interesting to us—is the way in which girls were educated and brought up. They were taught at home, sometimes by their mother and father, but more usually by governesses or masters. If Florence Nightingale's parents had wished to send her to a High School there were none in existence; if she herself had later wanted to go to a University not one would have admitted her. As it happened, her bent was towards training to be a nurse, but here also she found her path barred. English hospitals were then unsuitable places for girls and the nurses coarse, uneducated women from whom she could have learnt nothing.

INTRODUCTION

When once their education was 'finished' refined girls from well-to-do homes never left these homes except to marry and the idea of an 'independent career' was unheard of. So Florence Nightingale's life is particularly interesting since it shows how her own great ability and determination enabled her to rise above all these handicaps, make an independent life for herself and prove that women were capable of training for a profession. To her, as much as to any one woman, Englishwomen to-day owe their social and economic freedom. Thus while she may continue to be best known as the 'Heroine of the Crimea' we shall see that this was but one episode in a long life wholly devoted to public service and she will always remain one of the most outstanding women England has ever produced.

CHAPTER ONE

Childhood and Youth

In the beautiful Italian town of Florence there is a dignified house called the Villa Colombaia near the Porta Romana. It now has on one wall a plaque to commemorate the fact that Florence Nightingale was born there on 12th May 1820. Her parents had decided to make an extended foreign tour and both their daughters were born abroad. Travel was a leisurely affair in those days, for there were no railways and it was all done by carriage. If long distances were to be covered many weeks had to be spent in reaching places which would perhaps now be reached in as many hours. Florence's elder sister had been born in 1819 in Naples and had been called Parthenope, the ancient Greek name of that city, so it was perhaps natural that Mr. and Mrs. Nightingale should also have given their second daughter the name of her birthplace.

Mr. Nightingale had inherited the property of Lea Hall in Derbyshire from a great-uncle, Peter Nightingale (he had changed his name from William Edward Shore to William Edward Nightingale in 1815), and it was to Derbyshire, to this estate near Matlock, that the Nightingales turned their steps on returning from Europe with their two baby girls. When he got back from abroad Mr. Nightingale considered Lea Hall too small and decided to build, so the present dignified stone house, Lea Hurst, was

I

soon begun. It stands high with extensive views and has lovely grounds and gardens. A little later, in 1825, as Derbyshire was such a long way from London by carriage, Mr. Nightingale bought Embley Park near Romsey in Hampshire. The children spent most of the year in pleasant rural surroundings and it was certainly from her country upbringing that Florence got her love of nature. The usual arrangement was for the family to spend the winter at Embley Park and the summer at Lea Hurst, except for a few weeks in the spring when they went to London. In these two attractive homes the little girls grew up, learnt their lessons and (no doubt) planned their futures much like many other children of their own age. But in one respect they were luckier than other families, for they had parents who valued education for its own sake and did not regard it as merely the acquiring of 'accomplishments', and who superintended much of the teaching themselves. There was another influence, too, on their lives which was supremely important. This was that from both their father's and their mother's families they inherited a strong sense of what we now call 'social responsibility' which made them take an active interest in every effort to improve the condition and education of people less fortunate than themselves. Mrs. Nightingale had been before her marriage Miss Frances Smith, one of the eleven children of Mr. William Smith who had sat in Parliament for some forty years. He had been a great friend of William Wilberforce and other such men and had worked hard for many good causes, among them, that of the abolition of slavery. In Mr. Nightingale's family there was likewise a long tradition of public service. From the time that they were quite young, the two sisters must have heard

1. Embley Park, from a sketch by Parthenope Nightingale

Pub. by Bemrose & Son.   Derby & Mattock.

Lea Hurst, (near Mattock,)
the Home of
Miss Nightingale!

2. Lea Hurst

questions of great importance discussed in their parents' home, and who can tell how much of what she then heard influenced Florence in her later life?

Whether they were at Embley Park or at Lea Hurst the life of 'Parthe' or 'Pop', and 'Flo', as they were often called, was as utterly unlike that of children of the present day as it is possible to imagine. The first big difference perhaps was that, as six of Mrs. Nightingale's brothers and sisters were married and had families, they had a great many near relations. We have grown so used in this century to small families that it is difficult to imagine what it must have meant to Flo and her sister, as they had no brothers, to have such a delightful collection of boy and girl cousins. With some of them, especially with Hilary Bonham Carter and Marianne Nicholson (whose mothers were her mother's sisters) Florence was very intimate and they were her lifelong friends. One family of 'double' first cousins were particularly beloved, for they were the children of Mr. Nightingale's only sister, Mary Shore (called affectionately 'Aunt Mai') who had married Mrs. Nightingale's brother, Samuel Smith. Florence was specially devoted to Aunt Mai's baby son, William Shore, who was eleven years younger than herself. She always called him 'her' boy, treated him as though he were her own little brother and rejoiced whenever she had him at her home. Her cousin Hilary also had a baby brother, and some quaint childish letters have survived in which these two 'little mothers' compared notes about 'their babies' and how they were getting on. As he grew older Shore always spent part of his holidays with the Nightingales, and Florence's interest in and affection for him grew ever stronger. Besides this the Nightingale girls often went to pay visits to their uncles and aunts, and return visits were paid to Embley Park and Lea Hurst by the different relations. All these families had large comfortable country homes in which big parties could be invited to stay for long periods. When the various cousins were in the house they perhaps shared the Nightingale children's lessons and of course joined in any amusements that were provided.

The second very big difference from to-day was that neither Parthenope nor Florence ever went to school. There were no day schools near either of their homes to which Mrs. Nightingale would have wished her girls to go, and the idea of sending them to boarding school never seems to have arisen. Although there were many 'Young Ladies' Academies', few boarding schools could then have given them the broad education that they would get at similar schools to-day, though their first cousin, Hilary, did later go to one near Liverpool. So Parthe and Flo did their lessons at home with various governesses and masters. One governess, Miss Christie, was much beloved by Florence and she was heartbroken at her death a few years afterwards. They seem to have learnt the usual subjects, Scripture, English, writing, English history and arithmetic, that any children would have done at that date and most likely were taught from the usual lesson books. They also learnt to sew and to do fancy work. It was when they were rather older that their education became wider than that of most children. They had lessons in foreign history and the political history of England, Mr. Nightingale himself taught them Greek and Latin and they also studied mathematics. All these were very unusual subjects for girls to master in those days. They learnt to sing and play the piano, for no well-bred girl would have been considered 'properly educated' unless she had done so. When she was older Florence was an accomplished pianist and passionately fond of music. While of course such a subject as science would not have been considered necessary in their education, Parthe and Florence studied more foreign languages than any girl would ever be taught in a modern school. They learnt, besides French, both German and Italian, and could write these three languages as well as read and speak them fluently. Florence must have begun French when very young, she could always practise talking it with her French maid, Agathe, for when she was about eight or nine she began a diary in French, 'La Vie de Florence Rossignol', and continued it for a couple of years. The picture of it on page 6 will show you what a large bold handwriting she already had. It is written in ink and has always been carefully preserved.

When they were not doing their lessons Parthe and Florence had no organized games, like hockey or even lawn tennis, such as girls would play now, but they had ponies and became good riders and at both their country homes there were endless opportunities for country rambles and nature study. The routine of schoolroom life was interrupted at intervals by visits to London. While there, they sometimes had teaching by special masters. They also had the fun enjoyed by any children at any date of seeing the 'sights' of London and of going to places of entertainment. They visited St. Paul's and Westminster Abbey, and on one memorable night they went with all their cousins to Vauxhall, an amusement park that was closed long ago, and had a rapturous evening seeing the great crowds and marvelling at the illuminations.

From her very early girlhood Florence Nightingale

mde Marsh. Les deux dernières la
soutenaient; pendant que les six
autres tiraient son bras pour
remettre les os à leurs places. Je
crois que l'opération dura un quart-
d'heure; et elle criait cette pauvre
demoiselle, car cela lui faisait horrible-
ment mal, et nous qui étaient enfermés
sans chandelle, nous pleurions. Enfin,
cela cessa, et mde Marsh vient nous
dire en pleurant que tout était fini. L
que mde C. nous demandait; nous

sommes allés; elle était assise dans
un grand fauteuil, car elle s'était presque
trouvée mal : nous avons vu Horton,
qui disait que cela lui perçait le cœur
d'entendre crier mlle Christie. Cette même
nuit Clémence a couché avec elle, et elle
ne dormit pas du tout; son bras lui
faisait tant de mal. Le lendemain elle
s'est levé à trois heures de l'après-midi;
et tous les jours elle allait de mieux en
mieux, et en se levant se meilleur
heure, le médecin venant la voir de

1. Florence Nightingale's Diary, 1828

seems to have shown, if one can judge from her diaries and her letters, two characteristics which were very pronounced in later life. The first was her keen and exact power of observation and the other was her interest in sick people and her desire to help them. The fact that she observed very accurately what she saw, and methodically made a note of it, is shown not only in her diaries but in a letter she wrote when she was about ten, describing a visit she had paid to London, to her uncle, Octavius Smith, whose home was near his distillery at Millbank on the Thames.

'I went up into the distillery to the very tip-top by ladders with Uncle Oc Saturday night. We walked along a great pipe. We have had a good deal of boating which I like very much. We see three steamboats pass every day, the *Diana*, the *Fly* and the *Endeavour*.'

These diaries did not include the French diary already mentioned, but were journals in which Florence recorded her thoughts and reflections as well as the events of each day. At the present time few if any young girls would write down their thoughts in this way, but in Victorian times it was quite usual for them to do so. It is in these various diaries that we get sidelights on what Florence was thinking about and what she hoped to do. Her wish to be 'useful' to the sick seems to have come very early. A touching story is told that her first 'patient' was a collie called Cap who belonged to her father's shepherd. The poor dog had broken his paw and his master thought that he would never get well but Florence begged to be allowed to nurse him. She bandaged him up so successfully and cared for him so tenderly that in the end he recovered. Florence seems to have been unusually interested

7

in everything to do with illness, and it is curious that the very earliest thing that exists in her handwriting is a copy of a prescription. On the page of the French diary which is illustrated she gives a long account, with no important detail omitted, of how her dear Miss Christie had her dislocated shoulder set. It would probably be far-fetched to say that all these things 'prophesied' the career of the future heroine of the Crimea but it does at least show that Florence had perhaps a keener sympathy than most little girls of her age with other people's troubles, coupled with a strong desire to help them. When she was somewhat older she frequently went with her mother, both at Lea Hurst and Embley Park, to visit any villagers who were ill or needed help, for Mrs. Nightingale was a conscientious and charitable woman who thought, like all ladies of that time, that it was her duty to do so.

There was another matter on which in after years Florence was quite definite and that was that she had had a divine 'call' when quite young. This conviction of having been 'specially chosen' was not confined to Florence Nightingale, for many other women of deep religious feeling have had the same spiritual experience. She had been brought up in an intensely pious atmosphere and was herself very devout, so it is perhaps quite natural that she had this sense of a dedicated life. In her diary, when she was almost seventeen, she noted that 'God called me to His Service on February 7th, 1837,' but she remembered that she had had this consciousness of inner guidance far earlier. Some years afterwards she wrote: 'The thoughts and feelings that I have now I can remember since I was six years old. . . . The first thought I can remember, and the last, was nursing work.' The thing that troubled her,

8

both when she was a young girl and indeed until much later, was that she was uncertain what form her 'call' was to take or what her mission in life really was to be.

The year 1837, when young Queen Victoria came to the throne, was a landmark in the lives of the two Nightingale girls. Parthe was eighteen and Florence almost grown up and they had received an education which had been, as we have seen, much fuller than that of most girls of that time. As Mr. Nightingale wanted to make extensive alterations to Embley Park, he and his wife decided that it would be a good moment to take their daughters abroad to finish their education and have the advantages of foreign travel. We can guess that they were as much excited as any girls would be at the prospect of their very first trip abroad; there was a great flurry of preparation and packing and it seemed as though they never could be ready. It was so difficult, for one thing, to know what books to take, for they were to be away a long time and everyone recommended something different—and Parthe *must* have her sketching materials, for she was a keen and talented amateur artist, as we can see from the attractive drawing of her home which is reproduced on Plate 1.

In the end all was prepared and they set off on 8th September 1837, a party of six, Mr. and Mrs. Nightingale, Parthe and Florence, the girls' old nurse Mrs. Gale, and a French maid. They crossed over from Southampton to Havre and, like tourists to-day who take their cars, they also took their own conveyance, but it was a travelling carriage. In this they proceeded by comfortable stages to the South of France. The Nightingales did not take their own horses of course, but followed the usual custom of hiring, at the regular halts, post-horses with postillions to ride them. The English carriage must have been unusually heavy, for sometimes (so Florence tells us) Mr. Nightingale was forced to hire six horses instead of four. Florence and Parthe liked to travel in turns on the box seat where their father usually sat and they came inside willingly only when it was wet. The family spent almost a month at Nice and then travelled along the Riviera and by January 1838 were in Genoa. Italy at that time was not one united country as it is to-day, but was divided into eight states, each of which had certain differences of custom and government. Like many other foreign travellers the Nightingales had brought letters of introduction to various people in Genoa, and soon the girls had the opportunity of making many interesting acquaintances. And then there was such a lot to see and do. They visited all the museums and picture galleries and spent many happy mornings seeing the various beautiful churches. The sisters also had Italian lessons and Parthe had ample opportunities for sketching. In the evening they might perhaps go to a ball, or some other form of entertainment, and on one occasion they gave a very successful *soirée* themselves. But the most exciting evenings were those on which they attended a performance at the Opera. This was the first time either of the girls had had the opportunity of hearing any opera and they were in raptures over the various performers. What a treat it must have been to anyone as musical as Florence to hear the most famous singers of the moment—Grisi, Lablache, Rubini and many others. Their names are only names to us, but in 1838 these artists were as famous as any film star of the present day. 'I should like to go every night,' said Florence in her diary, and she kept one special note-book into which she put full details of each performance.

But Florence found an interest, even though she was not yet eighteen, in other things besides balls and parties. She seems even at that early age to have had a longing to know and see for herself how the less fortunate people worked and lived. This was quite consistent with her interest in nursing and she records in her journal how she visited a school for deaf-and-dumb children at Genoa. For Florence had not given up the habit of diary-keeping with 'La Vie de Florence Rossignol' and her other childish diaries; she wrote a very detailed account of all this foreign tour and made notes of everything she saw. Had it been anyone else's diary it might perhaps only have told us of museums and monuments and beautiful scenery, but because it is hers it is filled with comments on how people looked and how they were governed and whether there were proper arrangements for education or for the care of the poor and other such topics. She also showed her later passion for statistics by giving minute details of what distance they had covered each day, the state of the roads, what the inns were like where they put up for the night and many other such practical matters.

After Genoa the party moved on to Florence, where they spent two months. While there Florence Nightingale had a visit from her old *Balia*, an Italian peasant, who had been her nurse when she was a baby. In Florence, as in Genoa, the Nightingales had a full social life and met a great number of people. They also went the usual round of sightseeing. The sisters had some more instruction in Italian, as well as singing and drawing lessons.

Florence has a good deal to say about her native city,

but she seems really to have admired Genoa more. When they left Florence the Nightingales turned their faces northwards and decided to spend the summer in Northern Italy and in Geneva. This seems to have been a very happy time in all their lives and they met again a great many of the friends they had made in Genoa the previous winter. The lovely city of Geneva has always been a meeting-ground for different nationalities, and they found a number of outstanding people whose society they enjoyed. Geneva was such a success that they stayed there all through September and left for Paris early in October 1838.

At that time France was not a republic as at the present day, but a monarchy like England, the King being Louis Philippe. The Nightingales took an apartment right in the centre of Paris, at 22 Place Vendôme, and they all seem to have enjoyed it very much. When Florence wanted to keep up her journal or do any other writing she crept away to a flat behind their own, which was un-let, and found a room where she could be quiet. Of course, like any other English tourists, the Nightingales saw all that was interesting of the various 'sights' of Paris, but they were exceptionally fortunate in having the opportunity of making the acquaintance of some interesting and agreeable people. These introductions were chiefly due to a lady who, although she was more than twenty years older than Florence, was later to become one of her most intimate friends. Her name was Miss Mary Clarke and she and her mother had lived for many years in Paris and had a tremendous number of French friends. Mary Clarke seems to have taken an immediate fancy to the Nightingale girls and with her they went to many delightful parties in French families, and also were guests at others in the Clarkes' own flat where they met many distinguished people. They even had the rare privilege of being taken by Miss Clarke to the *salon* of the famous Madame Récamier. The friendship between Parthe and Florence Nightingale and Mary Clarke deepened every day and in later years this new friend became almost as intimate with Hilary Bonham Carter. In 1847 Miss Clarke married Monsieur Julius Mohl and continued to live in Paris, but her marriage made no difference to her friendship with Florence. She often came to stay with the Nightingales in England, both before and after her marriage, and Florence wrote her dozens of letters; in fact she was one of the few people in the years to come who seems really to have sympathized with, even if she could not entirely understand, her young friend's ambitions.

In April 1839, after being on the Continent for eighteen months, the whole Nightingale party came back to England. During their absence Embley Park had had extensive alterations and additions made to it—but unluckily it was not ready. The family did not, probably, want at that moment to go as far away as Derbyshire, so they went to London instead and stayed at the Carlton Hotel in Regent Street. Luckily for Florence her dear Marianne Nicholson was there also, and the two Nightingale girls and their pretty cousin were soon deeply engaged in the usual social round, and were presented at one of Queen Victoria's Drawing-rooms. They also had singing lessons and, in Florence's words, 'As Marianne Nicholson is as music-mad as I am we are revelling in music all day long'. Mrs. Nightingale had plenty to do meanwhile, for Embley Park had been made a good deal larger by the alterations (six bedrooms had been added) and she was kept busy choosing all the necessary furnishings. They finally got off to the country and spent the summer as usual at Lea Hurst. On their return to London Florence had, apparently, her first experience of railway travel, for she writes to Miss Clarke in September 1839: 'The next day we went up to town in six and a half hours notwithstanding that the engine was twice out of order and stopped us. . . . How much pleasanter it is travelling by these public conveyances than in one's own stupid carriage.' When they eventually got to Embley Park in September they found the workmen still in possession. Florence describes in a letter, evidently with great amusement, how they had to crawl into the house by candlelight and finally camp there even though it was not quite finished. But when once these discomforts were over they were delighted with the beauty of their Hampshire home, and a large family party assembled for Christmas in the transformed Embley Park. This was to be, Mrs. Nightingale felt, the perfect setting in which her daughters were to enjoy brilliant society and shine in it. Meanwhile, what was Florence thinking about it all?

CHAPTER TWO

Aspirations and Training. The Institute of Deaconesses at Kaiserswerth and the Establishment for Gentlewomen

If anyone had seen Florence Nightingale for the first time in that year 1839 when she was an attractive girl of nineteen he might have predicted for her a brilliant marriage, coupled perhaps with an important position and great influence on English society. There was nothing in her family or surroundings to suggest that any other sphere would be her destiny.

Florence was distinguished and elegant if not actually beautiful and must also have had that thing which every girl longs to possess—great charm. When she was young photography had not yet been invented, so we have only a few sketches and drawings to show us what she looked like. Several friends have however described her for us, for she was obviously one of those people who have an arresting personality and who, once met, are not easily forgotten. The American writer, Mrs. Julia Ward Howe, when she and her husband stayed at Embley at about this time, said of her: 'Florence was rather elegant than beautiful; she was tall and graceful of figure, her countenance mobile and expressive, her conversation most interesting,' and some years later Mrs. Gaskell wrote: 'She is tall: very straight and willowy in figure; thick and shortish rich brown hair; very delicate complexion; grey eyes, which are generally pensive and drooping, but when they choose can be the merriest eyes I ever saw; and perfect teeth making her smile the sweetest I ever saw.' In all pictures of Florence the most striking feature is the broad and lofty brow which gives her face a remarkable look of intelligence and distinction.

It must have seemed to everyone who knew the Nightingale family that Florence's lot was cast in very pleasant places and that she ought to consider herself an exceptionally fortunate girl. Her parents and her sister were devoted to her, she was very well off, she had a host of friends as well as the most delightful cousins, her family owned two beautiful homes, so what more, really, could the heart of any young girl desire? And at first Florence herself probably agreed with them. For a time, it seems, she was quite contented with this life of the well-bred Victorian young lady and did not try to look beyond it. In fact at one moment she felt that to 'shine in society' would be enough to make her happy, and in her private notes she confessed that she had a great desire to do so. She helped her parents to entertain their wide circle of friends at Embley Park and Lea Hurst and led in every way the life of the dutiful and agreeable 'daughter at home' similar to that of many other girls who are so vividly portrayed in novels of the period. She went to the usual round of parties and gaieties in London as well as in the country and seems to have been universally popular. The Christmas of 1841 found her at a large family gathering at Waverley, her aunt Mrs. Nicholson's home in Surrey. On Twelfth Night, the young people decided they would act *The*

Merchant of Venice, but they had left themselves very little time for rehearsing. Mrs. Nightingale described vividly in a letter to Miss Clarke how, while Parthe was busy painting the scenery and arranging the dresses, Flo had been selected as stage manager and contrived to discipline her rather unruly cast. She even persuaded one of her uncles to learn his part. Did any of that gay party guess, one wonders, that Flo's powers of organization and command were to be exercised not many years later in quite another sphere?

While pursuing this conventional social routine Florence, unlike some other young girls less clever and less well-educated than herself, read serious books in French and German as well as in English on many different subjects. Among her personal notes many extracts and précis exist to show the extensive range of her reading. In several exercise books she even copied out long passages which had impressed her. It was no doubt this continued training of her mind which gave Florence the mental grasp and power of concentration that were so remarkable in her later life. She was also much interested in all religious and philosophic questions as well as in contemporary politics and political history. Mr. Nightingale found her a congenial companion for, being himself of a reflective and philosophical turn of mind, it was with her rather than with Parthenope that he liked to indulge in religious speculation and discuss his political theories. The father and daughter were very close, and in after years it was to be he who was more sympathetic towards Florence's aspirations than either her mother or her sister. Perhaps she inherited many of her characteristics from her father and so they had much in common, but it was from her mother, who had what her daughter once called the 'genius for order', that she got her great powers of organization and her passion for method and accuracy.

But all the time that Florence was leading this conventional life of the young lady in society, a life no different from those of most of her contemporaries, she had never forgotten her 'call', nor those sick people whom she longed to help. She nursed her poorer neighbours in the cottages round Lea Hurst and Embley Park, although this was not always satisfactory for the regular moves of the family between their two homes made continuity of effort very difficult. Early in 1846 she wrote: 'I am almost heartbroken to leave Lea Hurst. There are so many duties which lie near at hand, and I could be well content to do them there all the days of my life. I have left so many poor friends there whom I shall never see again, and so much might have been done for them.' It is also true that Florence was the person to whom every member of her large circle of relations turned when there was sickness in the home. We hear of her nursing Grandmother Shore, her father's mother, in 1845, and in the same year she tended her old nurse Mrs. Gale in her last illness. There is a striking proof that the care of the sick was never far from her thoughts. Dr. Elizabeth Blackwell, the pioneer American woman doctor, tells us that when she was staying with the Nightingales at Embley in April 1851, and was strolling in the garden with Florence she had said: 'Do you know what I always think when I look at that row of windows? I think how I should turn it into a hospital, and just how I should place the beds.' As early as 1844 Mrs. Ward Howe records that on that same visit to Embley, Florence had taken Dr. Howe aside and asked him: 'If I

should determine to study nursing, and to devote my life
to that profession, do you think it would be a dreadful
thing?' He had replied: 'Not a dreadful thing at all; I
think it would be a very good thing.' The memory of
these words from one who was well known as a philan-
thropist must have been an encouragement to Florence in
the struggles that were to follow. It is very interesting
that she should have used the expression 'study nursing',
for she was quite clever enough to realize that merely
looking after her relations or tending the sick people in
the village was not really the way to learn how to be a
good nurse. She gradually began to feel that she must, in
some way or other, get some training. It is probably one
of the greatest proofs of Florence Nightingale's remarkable intellect that she seems to have grasped while in her
twenties a principle that most women of her time utterly
ignored, and that was: if you want to do anything properly you must *learn how to do it.* This principle seems now
so self-evident that we regard it as perfectly extraordinary
that most people at that date had not recognized it, but
any talk of 'training for a career' would have meant
nothing to girls of Florence's day. There were no careers
for them to follow—so what was the use of training and
what did 'training' mean anyhow? Many young ladies
that Florence saw around her were 'very accomplished',
as the saying went, and some were extremely well-read
and even learned, but Florence felt that what she was
seeking for was quite a different thing. Many years later,
when already an elderly woman, she remembered her
early difficulties and showed how strongly she still felt
about the subject by saying: 'Thirty years ago, if a girl
wanted training there was none to be had. I can truly say

that there was no training to be had to fit a woman thoroughly for any life whatsoever.' She never changed her convictions on this subject for, even later, in another connection, she said: 'Three-fourths of the whole mischief in women's lives arises from their excepting themselves from the rules of training considered necessary for men.' As Florence was determined to learn how to be a good nurse, she felt that the best way of doing this would be to go into a hospital. It was obvious to her that this was the right way and this again is equally obvious to us, but it was not at all obvious to her family. Each year that passed she felt keenly how the poor especially suffered from their friends' ignorance and said in a letter: 'I saw a poor woman die before my eyes this summer because there was no one but fools to sit up with her, who poisoned her as much as if they had given her arsenic.'

Florence remembered Dr. Howe's encouraging remarks and boldly suggested to her parents in 1845, when she was already twenty-five, that she should go into Salisbury Infirmary to get some training. She softened the blow by adding that she only wanted to go for a few months and that she needed this practical experience to be a better nurse to the poor people round Embley. The suggestion was received with absolute consternation by the whole family. They were at first too paralysed with astonishment to speak, but soon began to voice their objections. Hospitals were fearful places; she would both hear and see things which *no nice* girl ought ever even to think about, much less know about—in fact the whole idea was preposterous and absolutely out of the question. When she was quite an old lady, Florence said of this episode: 'It was as though I had wanted to become a kitchen-maid.' So she had to submit, for even the doctor's wife, Mrs. Fowler, who probably knew more about the Infirmary than either Mr. or Mrs. Nightingale, was entirely against the idea. Florence gives bitter expression to her disappointment in a letter to her dear Hilary, but there was nothing to be done. It is interesting to observe that Florence never seems to have questioned that she owed obedience to her parents; she was not so 'modern' that she wished deliberately to defy them. An added reason for the family disapproval may have been that in the previous year, 1844, Charles Dickens had written *Martin Chuzzlewit* in which there were two very unflattering pictures of hired nurses. When we read *Martin Chuzzlewit* now, at this distance of over a century, we may regard the descriptions of Mrs. Sairey Gamp and Mrs. Betsy Prig as grossly exaggerated, but perhaps we should make a mistake. Dickens, like all writers, must be allowed a little 'artistic licence', but he did not mean these portraits to be caricatures. Twenty-four years later he called Mrs. Gamp 'a fair representation of the hired attendant on the poor in sickness' and Mrs. Betsy Prig 'a fair specimen of a hospital nurse'. In view of these facts, Mr. and Mrs. Nightingale's objections can be readily understood, and we can fully sympathize with their desire to shield their adored daughter from what they knew would be a revolting environment.

Florence had no doubt also read *Martin Chuzzlewit*, but perhaps her reactions to Mrs. Gamp and Mrs. Prig were rather different. What filled other readers with disgust she may have regarded as a direct challenge to her to improve nursing so much that Gamps and Prigs would give place to respectable well-trained women. After this time we never

hear again of her trying to go into an English hospital to
train, but the subject of nursing was never far from her
thoughts. She was also more determined than ever to get
some kind of training but the question was—where? This
remained such a fearful problem that she could at the
moment see no solution. It was perhaps about then that
her thoughts turned inwards; the outside world saw only
the agreeable and charming young lady of the world, but
the *real* Florence was putting into her private note-books
all that she felt and dreamed of and they were often sad
reflections. She seems gradually to have become more and
more spiritually estranged from her family and the dom-
estic tension was very marked. Her greatest comfort was
perhaps in writing to Miss Hannah Nicholson, 'Aunt
Hannah', who was the sister of Mr. Nicholson, her uncle
by marriage. To her Florence poured forth her doubts
and difficulties and thoughts on religion, while Miss
Nicholson on her side gave endless comfort and moral
support to her unhappy young friend.

There is a saying that the darkest hour comes just before
the dawn and it happened that a small ray of hope illum-
ined the gloom of Florence's thoughts. The Prussian ambassador of the day was Baron von Bunsen, and he and
his family were friends of the Nightingales. It is believed
that his daughter showed Florence in about 1846 the
Annual Report of a German institution that had been in
existence for some time. As this Deaconess Institute of
Kaiserswerth was to have great influence on Florence
Nightingale's subsequent career it is necessary to give a
brief account of it. About twenty years before Florence
heard of the Institute, a young German Lutheran pastor
had come to England to beg for financial help for his

parish of Kaiserswerth on the Rhine which was in acute distress. His name was Pastor Theodor Fliedner and he got in touch with many influential people, among them the famous Elizabeth Fry of whose wonderful work for prisoners he had heard with admiration. Many English people sympathized with him and his list of subscribers was headed by the little Princess Victoria, the future Queen. When he got back again to Kaiserswerth, Pastor Fliedner and his first wife, Friederike, wanted to follow Mrs. Fry's good example, so they started a refuge for a few discharged prisoners. His desire to improve the welfare of prisoners was soon followed by a determination to do something to help the poor when they were ill, so he took a small house and converted it into a hospital. Like Florence herself he felt that some better class of women was needed in this hospital than the servant-nurses who were of quite as low a type in Germany as in England. He and his wife had therefore invited a few respectable young women to come and train as Deaconesses, thus reviving this ancient Church order. Within the next few years the Fliedners had also opened an orphanage and an infant school. All these different establishments were staffed by the Deaconesses, both those in training and those who were already consecrated. Pastor Fliedner and his wife managed the whole Institute themselves, the Pastor being responsible for the Deaconesses' moral teaching and religious instruction, while Friederike undertook their practical training.

When Florence Nightingale read these reports she must have felt that she had met, on paper at least, a kindred spirit. Here was something to which there was no parallel in England; here was somewhere where, surely, as it was a religious establishment run by a pastor and his wife, her relations could not disapprove of her going to train. From this moment all her thoughts turned towards Kaiserswerth, and she says about it in a private note-book: 'There is my home; there are my brothers and sisters all at work. There my heart is, and there I trust one day will be my body.' But in actual fact it proved to be four long years before she managed to go there. If reading about Pastor Fliedner's work made Florence more happy, since she knew that there was at least *one* place where she might find what she was looking for, yet on the other hand it increased her restlessness and her revulsion against what she felt to be the futility of her way of life. Into her private notes went her longings and hopes, her frustration and disappointment. She could tell Aunt Hannah and her dear Hilary something of what she felt, but neither of them could fully sympathize with all her misgivings and her doubts, nor, above all, could they understand why she wanted to be a nurse. Even her own family noticed how out of spirits she seemed, though they could not guess the real reason, and her health was definitely affected by her mental stress. So foreign travel was suggested as a cure. Whether it 'cured' her or not this journey did have a great effect on Florence's after-life, though not perhaps quite the effect her relations had anticipated. She had not been abroad for nearly ten years and her great friends, Mr. and Mrs. Bracebridge, invited her to go with them to Rome, where they were planning to spend the winter. Mrs. Bracebridge was one of Florence's closest friends and her unchanging affection and sympathy were to be one of Florence's greatest sources of happiness; indeed she remarked: 'I wonder whether she knows what a difference she has made in my life?' She accepted the invitation with enthusiasm and they were off by October. Unlike present-day travellers they arrived at Rome by sea, crossing from Marseilles to Civita Vecchia. It seems curious to us, when members of a family are now often separated for many years and are not so dependent on one another, that Parthe should have felt that this was a great milestone in her sister's life and should have written to a friend: 'Though it is but for so short a time, yet it seems to me a great event, the solemn first launching her into life.'

In 1847 Rome was the capital not of united Italy as it is to-day but of the Papal State, the Pope at that time being Pius IX. Many English people came to spend long periods there and the travellers when they arrived found quite a colony of their fellow-countrymen of whom several were their acquaintances. When English people are abroad they are naturally thrown a good deal into each other's company, and with two among their circle, Sidney Herbert and his wife, Florence Nightingale made a lifelong friendship. The Honourable Sidney Herbert was the second son of the eleventh Earl of Pembroke, and in the previous year had married Elizabeth à Court. He was a man of remarkable character and ability combined with an attractive personality and great charm of manner. In 1832 he had been elected the Member of Parliament for South Wiltshire, and in 1845, in Sir Robert Peel's government, had been made Secretary at War (an office that is now obsolete) with a seat in the Cabinet. This was the post to which he was later to return when Lord Aberdeen became Prime Minister. In 1846 Peel's government resigned and so Sidney Herbert was momentarily free from official work. Florence also met Archdeacon Manning, later the well-known Cardinal Manning, who in subsequent years helped her in many ways. Sidney and Elizabeth Herbert were deeply interested in every kind of charitable work and also in hospitals, and were planning to build one near their home, so Florence found them friends after her own heart.

Rome has always been one of the most beautiful cities in the world, but in those days it had a picturesqueness and an old-world charm that it has since lost. With the dear Bracebridges Florence saw all the interesting sights and read many books about Roman history. She recorded all her impressions in her journal (for on this journey too she kept a diary) and described all the wonderful places they visited. Besides studying ancient history, Florence seems to have taken as keen an interest in contemporary Italian politics. The revolutionary movement was at its height and she records all the hopes and fears of the party who were even then striving for a united Italy.

It was during this winter also that Florence Nightingale saw and studied for the first time the active Roman Catholic Sisterhoods for whose work she always felt great admiration. One of the most conspicuous landmarks in Rome is the convent of the Trinità dei Monti at the top of the famous Spanish steps. The nuns of the convent ran an orphanage and a school and after her introduction to the Madre Santa Colomba, who was in charge of the school, Florence was able to study these establishments. A little later she was permitted by the Mother Superior to go into Retreat at the convent. The Madre Santa Colomba had a profound influence on Florence; what she learnt from her she never forgot and she filled many note-books with her impressions. This winter was certainly an important landmark in her career and in after years she said: 'I never enjoyed any time in my life so much as my time at Rome.'

When Florence got home again she received a rapturous welcome from her family, the sort of welcome that is given to any traveller who has been away for some months and has much to tell of her adventures. But when this first excitement had worn off it was only too painfully clear that this long journey had not 'cured' Florence in the least of her curious ideas and of that unaccountable longing she had to be a nurse. What *was* to be done with such a girl, a daughter who did not openly rebel and who could still always be counted upon to be, at least outwardly, the model hostess but who was really, had they but realized it, a seething mass of revolt and frustration. The lack of understanding between Florence and her mother and sister became greater every day and she was more and more conscious of spiritual isolation. Those about her then hoped that she would find the solution to all her difficulties in a perfect marriage. It was apparently not an idle hope, for there had been several men who wanted to marry her although she does not seem to have really cared for any of them. There was one man, however, by whom she was, for a time at least, seriously attracted, and for whom she felt, if not love, at least great admiration and a conviction that they were in many ways very congenial. This was the poet Richard Monckton Milnes, afterwards Lord Houghton, who belonged to the same circle as herself. She had met him frequently and he had been to stay at Embley. But although Florence ultimately refused him it was a tremendous sacrifice and for many years she felt acutely the want of his companionship. She made this final decision not to marry because she felt that she must be free to devote her life to her ideal. What makes it all the more remarkable that she had the fortitude to make this choice is that, while she felt absolute certainty about her vocation, she did not know at all whether she would ever be able to follow it.

It seems likely that her family were even more paralysed with astonishment and scarcely less horrified that she did not choose this marriage than they had been when she had clamoured to go into Salisbury Infirmary, and the gulf between them gradually deepened. Florence Nightingale's whole life is one of the saddest examples of the fact that those who are closest to us in relationship often understand us least. Sometimes people would have us think that she took pleasure in being entirely at variance with her parents; in actual fact she deferred to their wishes until she was over thirty. What is far nearer the truth is that although she never openly rebelled, she was heart-broken over the lack of understanding shown by the mother and sister whom she loved so much. Indeed she once wrote about her mother: 'When I feel her disappointment in me, it is as if I was becoming insane.' The two sisters were very different in character and disposition and, although truly devoted to one another, they were also never really congenial, and Parthe summed it up in the phrase: 'The natures God gave us differ as widely as different races.' Perhaps Flo found it harder to bear that Parthe should be so utterly unable to understand, far less to sympathize with, her longings than that her parents should oppose her. After all, Parthe was her own age and those of the same generation *ought* to have seen eye to eye even if in fact they did not. In all these years of inner conflict and spiritual loneliness there were only three people besides Aunt Hannah to whom Florence could turn for sympathy, her dear Aunt Mai, her cousin Hilary and Mary Mohl. These years are full of letters to them which show her bitterness of mind and the unhappiness she was going through. She felt that there was no purpose in her life and must often have questioned how it would all end. Her communings with herself have sometimes almost a morbid note as when she writes, in December 1850: 'O weary days, O evenings that seem never to end! For how many long years I have watched that drawing-room clock and thought it would never reach the ten! And for twenty or thirty more years to do this! . . . In my thirty-first year I see nothing desirable but death.' She must have wondered which was the greater sorrow, the resentful disapproval of her parents or the incredulous lack of sympathy of her friends. The only thing she seems really to have enjoyed was teaching in one of the Ragged Schools for destitute children recently started in London by Lord Ashley.

So the year 1848 ended and part of 1849 passed by, and once more the dear Bracebridges were going abroad and once more they asked Florence to accompany them. They had seen how delightful a travelling companion she could be and they also, like most of her friends, had still the hope that she would regain her poise and happiness by a change of scene. This time the travellers journeyed farther afield. They went to Egypt and while there hired a dahabieh, and in this special Egyptian ship went up the Nile to the Cataracts. It must have been a wonderful journey and all the time of her travels Florence wrote long letters home to her family. She made quite a study of the history and religion of ancient Egypt, but appears to have been equally interested, as she had been while in Italy two years

before, in the lives of the modern Egyptians, and whenever the boat stopped she went into the villages and
'poked about', to use her own phrase. What interested
her perhaps more than anything was her visit to the
French Sisters of Charity at Alexandria. She gives a vivid
account of the work of the Sisters and says admiringly:
'Nineteen Sisters did the work of ninety.' Perhaps the
sight of these Sisters reminded her of the nursing work she
still so ardently wished to do, for she notes in her diary:
'O God, Thou puttest into my heart this great desire to
devote myself to the sick and sorrowful. I offer it to Thee.
Do with it what is for Thy service.'

From Egypt the travellers went on to Greece, and
Florence revelled in the beauty of Athens. After this they
went slowly back again to Europe. The climax of the tour
was, to Florence's way of thinking, the glimpse she was to
get of Kaiserswerth on her way home. Her parents had,
perhaps reluctantly, given their consent and she was
allowed to visit it. To us in this century it seems curious
that a woman of thirty should have needed permission
from her parents to do anything so decorous, but one
must remember that daughters were then, if they did not
marry, utterly dependent, both financially and in other
respects, on their families and Florence had no wish to
wound her parents unnecessarily. So to Kaiserswerth she
went and it quite came up to all that she had heard and
read about it. She lived in the Institution for a fortnight
and was allowed to see every part of the work. In fact she
was so much impressed with what she saw that she at once
wrote an account of it which she called The Institution of
Kaiserswerth on the Rhine, and while the party were still
abroad the dear Bracebridges helped her to correct the

manuscript. On returning to England she had it printed without putting her name to it and distributed copies among her friends. Why she wished the pamphlet to be anonymous one cannot now know; perhaps it was out of deference to her parents' feelings as they might have been annoyed at their daughter's showing in print an enthusiasm over something which they did not want for her. It is probable that Florence had a further object in view in writing about Kaiserswerth, namely a hope that if she publicized the work of this institution she might make people so enthusiastic about it that they would start some similar good work in England. It may have been this Kaiserswerth visit that strengthened Florence's resolve to have an independent life and she was quite determined to go there again and for an adequate period of training. The next year she got her way and went to Kaiserswerth from July to October while Mrs. Nightingale and Parthe were doing a cure at Carlsbad. Even then, although she had got her parents' consent, she had to contend with misgivings and doubts on her mother's part. Mrs. Nightingale seems to have been almost ashamed that Florence should be doing something so unlike what most women of her class would ever want to do, coupled with a feeling of reluctance to admit to her friends where Florence was. But on this point Florence was adamant; she argued with her mother that most of their circle of acquaintances would not know where she was anyhow and that their real friends who *did* know, such as the Herberts, the Bracebridges and the von Bunsens, would thoroughly approve. So Florence went to the Deaconesses and revelled in the Spartan life. In after years she always called it her 'spiritual home'. The régime at Kaiserswerth was a hard one and the time-table she sent her mother and sister while they were comfortably settled in their hotel at Carlsbad must have left them stunned.

'We have ten minutes for each of our meals, of which we have four. We get up at 5; breakfast ¼ before 6. The patients dine at 11.0, the Sisters at 12. We drink tea (i.e. a drink made of ground rye) between 2 and 3 and sup at 7. We have two ryes and two broths—ryes at 6 and 3, broths at 12 and 7; bread at the two former, vegetables at 12.' However, she added: 'The world here fills my life with interest and strengthens me in body and mind.'

But while her family wrung their hands with fear that Flo's health would never stand this life and were more than ever convinced that she really must be quite mad, the object of their sympathy was equal to the strain and was enjoying every moment in this inspiring place. For she found it in the best sense inspiring; she admired the religious atmosphere and the high moral tone and said, almost forty years afterwards: 'Never have I met with a higher tone, a purer devotion, than there.' Yet she never liked to hear it said, as people were apt to state, that she had received *all* her training in nursing at Kaiserswerth, for she considered the hospital work as the least good part of the Institution. It is significant, and goes to prove that she did not altogether admire the Deaconesses' nursing, that when, ten years later, she founded her own school, although she copied some things from Kaiserswerth she organized it on widely different lines and with a much higher professional standard. Nevertheless, although she had a few criticisms to make, this time at Kaiserswerth was the real turning point in Florence's life. She was never able to visit it again; possibly she felt that she had learnt all that they were able to teach her about nursing, but she kept in touch with the Fliedners for many years. It must have been an enormous encouragement to her after the lack of sympathy with which her ideas had been met, to find at least two religious and high-minded people, the Pastor and his wife, who did not think it at all reprehensible that she wanted to nurse, but welcomed her and gave her every opportunity of learning all she could. Yet she still craved for some sign of approval and understanding from her family in this work she had chosen, and wrote to her mother from the Deaconess Institute: 'I should be as happy here as the day is long, if I could hope that I had your smile, your blessing, your sympathy upon it.'

Had her family but known it, it was a different Florence that came back in 1851 to the family circle. She was more determined than ever to follow her vocation and the next year saw her making further attempts to supplement the training as a nurse that she felt she had only partially received at Kaiserswerth. She wrote to her friend, Dr. Manning, who had joined the Roman Catholic Church the previous year, and asked him if he could gain admission for her to the hospital in Dublin run by the Sisters of Mercy, a nursing order which had been started about twenty years previously and was doing devoted work among the poor. In her letter she bluntly stated the reason for this request: 'I want to be employed there at once, for it is not for purposes of retreat that I go . . . but to learn their trade.' A little later in the same year Florence visited Dublin and saw the Sisters' hospital, but her plan for going there never matured. Dr. Manning did not forget his earnest young friend and at the very beginning of 1853 she got, through his good offices, permission to work at the Maison de la Providence of the Sisters of Charity in Paris. She also obtained a general permit from the *Assistance Publique* of Paris to visit its establishments. The *Assistance Publique*, like the London County Council, had not only hospitals but various other institutions under its control. She went over in February 1853 to stay with her old friends, Monsieur and Madame Mohl, and from their home went round, armed with her permit, to visit as many of these institutions as she could include and made elaborate notes on their management. She had settled the day on which she was to go to the Maison de la Providence when she was hastily summoned back to nurse her Grandmother Shore, her father's mother. Florence at that time still put family ties before her own work, later on she was to reverse the process, and she nursed the old lady, who was ninety-five, until her death. It was a return to her old rôle of attending to any sick relation in her large family. Then on 30th May she went back to Paris and, after spending a week with the Mohls, eventually went to the Maison de la Providence on the 8th June. She was no doubt looking forward with thrilled anticipation to the interesting work she was going to do with the Sisters—when all her bright hopes were dashed by developing measles! As she had had the disease barely eighteen months before, it was, she felt, a most cruel joke of Fate that she should get it again and at such an inconvenient moment. When she was well enough to be moved she convalesced at the Mohls' home, and by the middle of July was back again in London. She was never able to return to the kind Sisters to finish her truncated training, for earlier in 1853 she had been negotiating with friends to become Superintendent of a small hospital in London.

Even during these negotiations her mother and sister tried to divert her from her purpose by proposing alternatives. Why could she not, they suggested, run some small institution of her own at Cromford Bridge House near Lea Hurst, or at Forest Lodge near Embley? But Florence was wise enough to see that she could not combine home life with an independent career and, although she was touched by the offer, she was more determined than ever to go to London.

There was at that time in Chandos Street, Cavendish Square, a small private hospital called the Establishment for Gentlewomen during Illness which had been started for governesses and other ladies of limited means. It was filling a real need, for its aim was to care for those who could not be admitted to the general hospitals and who would, consequently, have lacked any nursing. The Committee of Ladies included several friends of Florence Nightingale, among them Mrs. Herbert, and they felt that it was a post for which she would be peculiarly fitted. They felt, too, that the Nightingale parents could not object so strongly to her working in a small private home which would have none of the objectionable features of the ordinary hospital. Meanwhile, after Florence had accepted the post, new premises had to be found for the home and once they had been found at 1 Upper Harley Street the house needed considerable alterations. It was while these were being done that Florence had been able to go to Paris. It is very interesting to notice that Florence was deeply concerned with every detail of these alterations and insisted on several improvements. Among the things she considered essential was a lift 'to prevent the nurse becoming a pair of legs', as she vividly puts it. All these things we now consider such obvious necessities that we should take them for granted, but then they were quite novelties. By August 1853 the house was pronounced ready; she moved in on the 12th and admitted her first patients a day or so later.

When Florence Nightingale accepted the direction of the Establishment for Gentlewomen it was perhaps not exactly the work she had hoped for, but at least it was a beginning. She was now thirty-three and probably felt that she must not let this chance slip as this position might afterwards lead to something else. She found great happiness in her new life and in January 1854 wrote to Aunt Hannah: 'I begin the New Year with more true feeling of a Happy New Year than I ever had in my life.' Her father made her an allowance of £500 a year, a generous sum in those days, and this enabled her to work for the institution on a voluntary basis. She also brought with her a housekeeper, Mrs. Clarke, whose salary and other expenses she paid herself. For the first time in her life she found herself independent of her family and in charge of real patients and working for real doctors in a hospital that was, albeit very modest, a real hospital which filled a great need. In running it she also had the first opportunity of putting into practice all those theories as to how a hospital should be run that she had probably been forming for many years in her own mind. She also learnt, what she could never have done from any number of books or reports, how to work with people and get the best out of them. There is no doubt that this year in her life was a happy one and was of special value to her in the great work she was soon to do. We do not know many details of the time she spent in Upper Harley Street, for she had little leisure to write letters and few other records remain.

Yet there is ample proof that she did her work successfully and that both the doctors and the patients admired and
appreciated it. Some of the patients wrote to her after they
had left and a few of these letters still exist to show us how
they loved her and how grateful they were for her kindness.

Her mother and sister had now become resigned to
Florence's having an independent life of work and it was
to Lea Hurst that she went in the summer of 1854 for a
short change. When she heard that cholera had broken
out in London she curtailed her holiday, returned immediately, and went to the Middlesex Hospital to help nurse
the many extra cases. Of this particular short period in her
life we know scarcely more than the dates, but it must
have been valuable to her, for it gave her the first practical insight into what happened when a sudden emergency arose to dislocate the ordinary work of a large
hospital. This experience stood her in good stead a couple
of years later when she was struggling with the over-
whelming number of patients in the East.

The thing that Florence Nightingale probably felt to be
most lacking in her work at the Establishment for Gentlewomen was any opportunity of training other people.
Her greatest desire had always been, as we know, to train
women to become good nurses, and in this small hospital
she had no scope for teaching. Some of her friends wanted
her to have a wider field of work with more opportunity
for training others, and the Governors of King's College
Hospital (which was then near the Strand) were anxious
that she should become Superintendent of nurses. It is
recorded that she got as far as accepting the post, but
before she could go to King's an even greater piece of
work had been entrusted to her.

CHAPTER THREE

The Outbreak of the Crimean War

W
hen Florence Nightingale was back again at
Upper Harley Street in September 1854 and
busily at work, her great opportunity, could
she have foretold it, was near at hand. For years she had
longed for such a chance of service and had been uncon-
sciously preparing herself for it. In March 1854, England,
France and Turkey declared war on Russia and the first
hostilities in what is commonly called the Crimean War
soon took place. The fact that England was engaged in a
war must have made a considerable stir in the country,
for no British army had fought in Europe since the end of
the Peninsular War some forty years before. To those
families whose relations were in the armed forces the
Crimean War caused great distress and suffering, but it
did not bring to the life of every civilian the disturbance,
danger and anxiety that the Second World War brought
in so many countries. The fighting and the casualties were
hundreds of miles away and not on one's doorstep as in
1939.

On the other hand, the sufferings of the troops were
infinitely greater, since few measures were taken to re-
lieve them. One woman at least, Florence Nightingale,
had the imagination to realize what war really meant to
the soldier. Other people in England no doubt felt great

concern for the welfare of their fighting forces so far away, but most of them probably assumed that those in authority had done everything possible for their care. So it must have come as a fearful shock when by the end of September ugly rumours began to reach England of mismanagement in the military hospitals and neglect of the sick and wounded. At first what people heard were only rumours and no doubt many thought them unreliable, for rumours have a way of being spread in any war. But all too soon there were articles in the papers which proved that the rumours were, alas, for once the truth. The war correspondent of *The Times*, Mr. W. H. Russell, was not afraid to speak his mind and he described what he saw in no uncertain terms. He said on the 12th October that the military hospitals had not got 'the commonest appliances of a workhouse sick ward' and that 'the men must die through the medical staffs of the British army having forgotten that old rags are necessary for the dressing of wounds'.

At that time there were no women nurses regularly employed in British army hospitals and two days afterwards someone who had seen the good work done in the French military hospitals by the Sisters wrote in *The Times*: 'Why have we no Sisters of Charity?' Their excellent care of the French soldiers was obviously a novelty to Englishmen, for a little later the *Illustrated London News* published a picture of them at work in a ward of their hospital.

When the British public read these dreadful accounts by eye-witnesses, even those who had previously been unconvinced were speechless with indignation at this complete breakdown of army efficiency. There was one person who read the papers and felt stirred by the news as no one else and this person was Florence Nightingale.

Had her 'call' come, she wondered? Could it really be that *she* was to be the woman who was destined to go out and nurse the wretched soldiers? By great good fortune it happened that her friend, Sidney Herbert, was once more holding the office (now obsolete) of Secretary *at* War while the Duke of Newcastle was Secretary *for* War. On the 14th October she wrote to Mrs. Herbert offering her services in any capacity. Sidney Herbert was out of London, but on that very same day he wrote a private letter to Florence and the curious coincidence that their letters crossed in the post has often been pointed out. What his letter contained was a definite request that she should go out to the East and take with her a group of nurses to work in the military hospitals. Sidney Herbert and his wife knew Florence well and fully appreciated her exceptional ability, so he was not exaggerating when he wrote:

'There is but one person in England that I know of who would be capable of organizing and superintending such a scheme ... but I must not conceal from you that I think upon your decision will depend the ultimate success or failure of the plan.'

It is difficult for us to realize what a brave man Sidney Herbert was in suggesting such a scheme, for he was fully alive to the criticism his decision to send nurses was bound to meet. In 1854 army hospitals, as we have seen, had no regularly appointed women nurses, so to send them out would be an innovation that would amaze everyone and probably shock many people profoundly. But he felt it was his duty to take this revolutionary step, although perhaps neither he nor even Florence Nightingale herself realized that, because of this bold action, he was writing a new chapter in the history of English women

2. Map Illustrating the Crimean Campaign

by opening a new profession to them. If Sidney Herbert had not had this supreme courage the subsequent history of British nursing would have been very different.

Florence Nightingale did not hesitate for one moment to accept the offer and the committee of her hospital willingly released her for this important national service. It seems curious that even in the face of such an emergency and although she was already thirty-four she apparently felt a doubt as to whether her family would approve of her going. So her kind uncle, Samuel Smith, took all the trouble to travel to Lea Hurst to prepare her parents' minds and to obtain their consent, which for once was willingly given.

For the next few days Florence Nightingale's life was one incessant rush, for there was so much to do and only one short week in which to do it. She herself could settle her own affairs and pack up what she needed quite quickly, but it was to her that Sidney Herbert had entrusted the selection of the nurses who were to go with her, and to get suitable women was an almost impossible undertaking. If Florence had had a similar task in 1914 or in 1939 it would have been simple. She would have found plenty of well-qualified nurses from whom to choose and could also have appealed for help to the British Red Cross Society. But in 1854 there were no trained nurses and the B.R.C.S. was not started until 1870, so what was she to do? She knew perfectly well that most of the women working in English hospitals as nurses were uneducated, unreliable and possibly not even respectable, and the onerous task of choosing her staff was not made easier by the fact that the selection had to be made in such a hurry. It was then that she remembered the Roman Catholic

Nursing Sisterhoods whose work and discipline she had admired a few years before. She applied to the Sisters of Mercy, whose hospital she had visited in Dublin, as they had a branch house in London at Bermondsey. They willingly sent some of their Sisters, and nurses were also offered by St. John's House, a nursing institution of the Church of England which had been started in London six years before. It is a curious proof of how little even responsible people understood what nursing in military hospitals would really be like, that at first the authorities of St. John's House stipulated that their nurses must remain under *their* orders and not under those of Florence Nightingale, and even suggested that the clergyman who was Master of St. John's House should go with the party to be 'their guardian'! Eventually, after an interview between Florence Nightingale, Sidney Herbert, the St. John's Council and the Chaplain General of the Army, they were persuaded to withdraw this stipulation. Florence also applied to a society of lay nurses that had been started in 1840 by the famous Mrs. Fry, but the managing committee, like that of St. John's House, refused to allow any of their members to go if they were to be under Florence's sole orders and as they would not reconsider this decision none of their nurses went to Scutari. As Florence probably guessed the difficulties she might have, she wished to take at first only twenty nurses, but Sidney Herbert thought that there should be forty and in the end there were thirty-eight. There were ten Roman Catholic Sisters from Bermondsey and Norwood, eight Anglican Sisters from an order also called Sisters of Mercy that had been founded at Devonport by Miss Sellon a few years before, six nurses from St. John's House and fourteen lay nurses from different hospitals. The whole party of women numbered forty-one as Florence took Mrs. Clarke, the housekeeper from Upper Harley Street, and there were also Mr. and Mrs. Bracebridge who had offered to come with her and help her in any way they could. On the 19th October she received her official instructions from the Army Medical Department and on the 21st October they all left London on their great adventure. She was the accredited servant of the country, a position no woman had held before. When Florence was actually about to depart her parents seem to have felt as much gratification over their daughter's flattering appointment as they had before felt doubts and misgivings. Even Parthe, who had looked with such an unsympathetic eye on her sister's desire to nurse, now wrote to a friend: 'I must say the way in which all things have tended to and fitted her for this is so very remarkable that one cannot but believe she was intended for it.' From her mother Florence had a parting letter of loving good wishes, and both Dr. Manning and Monckton Milnes sent messages of encouragement. She must often have thought gratefully of this sympathy on her voyage to such an uncertain destiny.

During the first stage of their journey a touching story is told of how, when they got to Boulogne, the fisher-women felt so enthusiastic about the devoted work that these women were going to do that they insisted on carrying the nurses' baggage themselves. After a night in Paris they travelled to Marseilles, where Mr. Samuel Smith left them, and went on board the *Vectis* on the 27th October. They had an extremely rough passage and almost every-one except Mrs. Bracebridge was very seasick. Even Florence was as much prostrated as the rest. The *Vectis* had been built for cargo traffic, not for passengers, and the unfortunate nurses found themselves in cramped cold quarters with wretched food. Who can say whether some of them felt their patriotic enthusiasm ebbing away and wished that they had never come? However, on the 4th November they eventually reached the beautiful city of Constantinople (now called Istanbul) and everyone had by then recovered.

The city of Constantinople is divided into two parts by a narrow strait, the Bosphorus, the section on the European side being called Pera and that on the Asiatic side Scutari. The French hospitals were at Pera, but the British sick and wounded had been taken to Scutari. One can see to this day a huge square yellow building, built round a large courtyard and with a tower at each corner, that stands in a magnificent commanding position high above the Bosphorus. This was the Barrack Hospital in which Florence Nightingale spent most of her time in the East. It had not been built as a hospital but as barracks, and had been handed over by the Turkish Government to the British to accommodate their sick and wounded. There was another hospital, the General Hospital, which had been the Turkish Military Hospital, about a quarter of a mile away from the Barrack Hospital, and two others rather more distant. Florence was responsible for the nursing in these four hospitals and she knew that they were all by now full of patients. Unluckily, all these base hospitals were hundreds of miles from the actual scene of the fighting.

Between the Barrack Hospital and the Bosphorus straggled the squalid little town of Scutari. From it Pera could be reached only in a caique, or open row-boat, and the passage was often impossible in stormy weather. It was in some of these caiques that Mr. and Mrs. Brace-bridge, Florence herself and the party of nurses crossed over from Pera to Scutari and they then established themselves in one of the towers of the Barrack Hospital; in fact it was Florence's headquarters throughout the campaign. There was not really room for over forty people in this tower, and, besides being very inadequate, the available accommodation was cold, uncomfortable and dirty. The cramped and squalid conditions under which they were forced to live added greatly to the nurses' fatigue and made it difficult to keep up their morale, since they had no chance of relaxation when off-duty until Florence was able, in the following year, to get a house for some of them. To give her family at home an idea of how they were installed, she drew a rough plan of the 'Sisters' Tower', as it came to be called, and this shows that the Roman Catholic nuns had one room, the Sellon Sisters a second, the lay nurses a third, while Mr. Bracebridge and the courier slept in one tiny room and Florence and Mrs. Bracebridge in another. Outside these bedrooms there was a large anteroom which had to serve as a kitchen and also soon became filled with stores of all kinds. It was here that Mrs. Clarke presided over the distribution of jelly, beef tea, arrowroot, and other delicacies for which requisitions were made by the surgeons. There were also innumerable people of every nationality and language constantly passing in and out on different errands and it soon got the nickname of the 'Tower of Babel'.

The difficulties the little band of nurses encountered in making their living quarters tolerably habitable were as trifles compared with the difficulties they were to meet in the wards. No one welcomed them except the patients. Florence had, of course, been furnished by Dr. Andrew Smith, the Director-General of the Army Medical Department in London, with an official introduction to Dr. Edward Menzies. He was acting as Principal Medical Officer of the hospitals at Scutari, as at that moment Dr. John (afterwards Sir John) Hall was in the Crimea. It was under Dr. Menzies's orders that Florence and her nurses were to work. She also knew that Sidney Herbert had instructed Mr. Wreford, the Purveyor-General, to help her in every way. Yet neither Dr. Menzies, nor the army surgeons, nor indeed any of the officials, were pleased at the coming of the nurses, for the very fact that Sidney Herbert had thought it necessary to send them out implied that the War Office was not satisfied with the way in which the hospitals were being run. So some of the officials opposed Florence as much as they dared and behind her back made great jokes about 'The Bird' and all that she hoped to do. Some, on the other hand, seem to have had the sense to appreciate her work and helped her in every possible way; a few even became her firm friends. The Commander-in-Chief, Lord Raglan, wrote her, from his quarters before Sebastopol, a letter of encouragement. In Scutari the Senior Army Chaplain, Mr. Sabin, was also most helpful and said of her: 'Miss Nightingale is an admirable person; none of us can sufficiently admire her.' So even if the military officials obstructed her, Florence had many sympathizers and helpers who gave her their assistance in various ways. It is significant that during all her career she was able to rely on this devoted assistance from a large number of people.

What made many of the officials even less cordial in

their reception of Florence was that they were already smarting under the news of an impending investigation by the War Office. There had been such an outcry about the condition of the hospitals that the Secretary for War, the Duke of Newcastle, had dispatched a Commission of Enquiry and the three Commissioners, Dr. Cumming, Dr. Spence and a lawyer, Mr. Benson Maxwell, had arrived at the same time as Florence and her nurses. Dr. Cumming subsequently stayed on as Deputy Inspector-General of the hospitals.

When Florence went round the hospitals for the first time, a day or so after her arrival, to settle with her chief, Dr. Menzies, how the nurses were to be distributed, she saw at a glance that the accounts in the newspapers of the appalling conditions that prevailed and of the gross neglect of the patients were only too true. Everything, as *The Times* correspondent had truly observed, was lacking, and the wards were filthy and verminous. There were no bedsteads, no blankets, no sheets, no chairs, no forks, no plates—indeed there did not appear to be even any medical equipment. The poor soldiers lay in their dirty blood-stained uniforms without even shirts and their wounds had perhaps not been dressed for several days. A few decrepit Chelsea pensioners were their only attendants except for some orderlies who were utterly incompetent. 'A man is selected for an orderly', said a subsequent report, 'who does not fit well into the ranks, and who is an ugly or clumsy fellow.' The trouble, Florence quickly realized, had begun long before the men reached Scutari. In 1854 there were no air ambulances and even before arriving at the base hospitals the sick and wounded had had to endure a rough passage across the Black Sea lasting anything from six to eight days in an uncomfortable overcrowded boat. Sometimes there were not enough doctors or orderlies on board to attend to them and occasionally they had not even had enough food. In the four months since the beginning of the campaign, out of every thousand men that had embarked at Balaclava seventy-four had died on board. So they were often in a critical condition before they were disembarked, and the landing itself was difficult and very painful for men with severe wounds, as there was no proper pier at Scutari. The stretchers had to be brought down to where the transports were moored alongside a dilapidated landing-stage and from there the casualties were carried up the steep hill. When the weary stretcher-bearers did eventually reach the hospitals there were not enough beds to receive the patients and they were deposited on palliasses, a makeshift kind of mattress contrived by filling rough canvas bags with chopped straw. The climax of their misery was reached when it was found that there were not even bedsteads and that the palliasses had to be put straight down on to the cold floor.

But even worse was to come, and the exceptional abilities of Florence Nightingale were soon to be taxed to the utmost. On the very day after the nurses had arrived at Scutari, 5th November 1854, the battle of Inkerman was fought and she was warned that within a few days she might expect over five hundred more sick and wounded men to arrive in the already overcrowded hospital. This was a real challenge to her capacities, a challenge that was all the more rousing as the time for preparation was so short and there was so much to be done. It was then that her genius for organization asserted itself and her commanding spirit rose to meet this terrible emergency. All those years she had spent in studying hospitals and in training herself were now to bear fruit. But perhaps even she had not realized quite how difficult her task was to be, for so many demands on her were made simultaneously. She had to decide very quickly which were the most important of these demands, and how she could most profitably go beyond the duties laid down for her and assist in matters which were, strictly speaking, quite outside her province as Superintendent of Nurses. It was a situation demanding tact, initiative and persistence. Fortunately Florence possessed all these qualities in full measure. Above all, she had to be willing to take full responsibility for her actions, even though the officials might think them irregular. It is recorded how on one occasion at her own expense she got some Turkish workmen in to repair some much-needed wards after the officials had declared it to be 'quite impossible'.

The next great question was: what ought to be done *first*? The answer was to supply immediately the most glaring deficiencies in the hospitals. So her nurses were set down to make more palliasses at once, and one of the Sellon Sisters graphically records how hard they worked. Then the wards must be got clean—and how surprised the Purveyor must have been when he soon received a requisition for three hundred scrubbing brushes! This was only the first shock he was to endure, for Florence tells us: 'This morning I foraged in the Purveyor's store—a cruise I make almost daily, as the only way of getting things. No mops, no plates, no wooden trays (the engineer is having these made), no slippers, no shoe brushes, no blacking, no knives and forks, no spoons, no scissors (for cutting the men's hair which is literally alive), no basins, no towelling, no chloride of zinc.' This lack of stores was entirely contrary to what she had been officially told to expect. Before she had left England Sidney Herbert had assured her that the hospitals were well provided; he even used the phrase 'as to medical stores, they have been sent out in profusion'. Dr. Menzies had reported officially to his chief, Dr. Andrew Smith: 'I must inform you that our hospitals here are in first rate order as regards cleanliness and comfort.' Even the British Ambassador to Turkey, Lord Stratford de Redcliffe, had assured Mr. Macdonald, who had just come out to administer a fund started by *The Times*, that nothing whatsoever was needed in any hospital and that the money had better be applied to building an English church at Pera! Fortunately for the wounded men Mr. Macdonald was not so easily hoodwinked and he did what many harassed men were to do in the years to come—he went to Florence Nightingale to get her advice and to offer his services. He could not forget, and nor could she, that his paper had contained on the 12th October a sentence that read: 'What will be said when it is known that there is not even linen to make bandages for the wounded?' After this they became close allies and through *The Times* Florence was able to supply many things that were not 'nursing' in the strict sense as well as from her own resources. She had been sent money direct by many sympathizers and in the end her private fund amounted to about £7,000.

Another person who was also at Scutari at this moment was Sidney Godolphin Osborne, a clergyman, who was a constant contributor to *The Times*, signing his articles 'S. G. O.' He came out as a free-lance and arrived on the 8th November, only four days after Florence herself, on whom he called at once to offer his services. Mr. Osborne, who was soon working as an extra Chaplain in the hospital, was greatly impressed by Florence and wrote the following description of her which is all the more interesting as he was an unbiased observer who had had unrivalled opportunities of seeing her work. 'Miss Nightingale in appearance, is just what you would expect in any other well-bred woman, who may have seen perhaps rather more than thirty years of life; her manner and countenance are prepossessing, and this without the possession of positive beauty; it is a face not easily forgotten, pleasing in its smile, with an eye betokening great self possession, and giving when she wishes, a quiet look of firm determination to every feature. Her general demeanour is quiet and rather reserved; still I am much mistaken if she is not gifted with a very lively sense of the ridiculous. . . . She has trained herself to command, and learned the value of conciliation towards others, and constraint over herself.'

With Mr. Macdonald, Mr. Osborne and Mr. Bracebridge to help her, Florence had soon scoured the town of Pera for the obvious necessities of the men and had even got them hundreds of shirts. This last was a matter of such urgency that she wrote on the 7th November to the British Ambassador, only three days after her arrival: 'I beg to state that there is at present a great deficiency of linen among the men in the Hospitals until the Government Stores can arrive and be appropriated to them. A hundred pairs of sheets and two hundred shirts might be applied to such a temporary purpose and would never be *de trop.*' By these drastic measures Florence had soon collected quite an appreciable amount of equipment, but she knew that she should never have had to do it and she wrote: 'I always expected to end my days as a Hospital Matron, but I never expected to be a Barrack Mistress.'

The next most urgent duty, she felt, was to establish some sort of auxiliary kitchen, or 'Extra Diet Kitchen' as it was generally termed, where delicacies of all kinds and nourishing foods could be prepared for the patients who were critically ill. Nowadays we have grown so accustomed to the idea of special diets for invalids and special diet kitchens in which they are prepared, that it seems almost impossible to realize that there was nothing of the kind in the Barrack Hospital. Up to Florence's arrival the routine of feeding the two thousand and more patients had been as follows: A certain amount of meat was boiled (the army cooks had never heard of any other way of cooking it!) and portions of this boiled meat were taken to the wards. This took about two to four hours, for there was only one kitchen and the corridors were very long. In the ward it was then cut up and each patient got a portion, which might be good meat or might merely be gristle. If the soldier was able to sit up and eat it, well and good, but if not there was no one to feed him and the plateful remained slowly congealing at his bedside. If you want to know what this looked like, the film *The White Angel* gives you a good idea. Florence had no doubt seen those congealing platefuls in the wards where she was working and very soon determined to alter all this. She got two special kitchens established in different parts of the vast building in which extra diets and nourishing food could be prepared which the nurses could then take to those patients who needed them most. The ingredients of these delicacies she supplied herself from her own stores.

In April 1855 she acquired a very welcome co-worker in this particular work. Alexis Soyer, a Frenchman who had long been well known in London as the chef of the Reform Club, came out from England and took over this department, thus relieving Florence of a great deal of responsibility. Soyer was a picturesque figure who did a great deal to improve the ordinary diet of the soldiers as well as to raise the general standard of the cooking both at Scutari and afterwards in the Crimea itself. It was he who subsequently invented the 'Soyer' stove for cooking in the open which is still used on active service in the British Army. Later on he wrote an entertaining and vivid book about his experiences called *Soyer's Culinary Campaign* which tells us a great deal about Florence Nightingale for whom he had a profound admiration.

Another very urgent need was to tackle the problem of providing clean linen, and Florence quickly got a laundry started for the hospital. Before she came only six shirts had been washed in a month by the fraudulent civilians who had contracted to perform this service, and even these could hardly be called 'washed', as all the 'washing' had been done in cold water and with scarcely any soap. One batch of linen handled in this way, although called 'clean', was so full of vermin that it had to be destroyed. So she took a house near by at her own expense, got the Royal Engineers to install a boiler and employed the soldiers' wives in this essential hospital service.

The care of these women was another burden laid on Florence which has, of course, no modern parallel. In those days soldiers were allowed to take their wives with them on campaigns, but no provision was made for these poor women and their families once they had left England, and they were glad to earn some money in this way. Florence's attention had been drawn to their deplorable condition by the Chaplain, who begged her to allow one of the nurses to come with him and see what could be done to help a woman who was very ill. Florence demurred, because she had been sent out to nurse the soldiers, not to care for their dependants, so although she felt profound sympathy for them she knew that she must entrust someone else with their care. This was a sphere where private charity could be responsible for what could not be undertaken from official sources. So she sent for Sister Sarah Anne, one of the Sellonites, to do what she could. Her tale of the destitution of these poor women was so piteous that Florence begged Mrs. Bracebridge to look after them. Later on Florence had a voluntary helper, Lady Alicia Blackwood, who had come out with her husband to do any work she could. He was a clergyman and was also soon acting as an Assistant Chaplain. Lady Alicia afterwards wrote her reminiscences, and her account of her first interview with Florence is interesting because it shows how, although anxious to find help for these unfortunate women, Florence was unwilling (as always) to have assistance from someone who had merely a sentimental motive. Lady Alicia said to Florence: 'What work needs doing?' 'Do you mean what you say?' said Florence. 'Yes, certainly', Lady Alicia replied, 'I am in earnest, and we came out here with no other wish than to help.' 'Very well,' said Florence, 'you can help me with the soldiers' wives'—and then went on to tell her what Sister Sarah had seen. Soon after this Lady Alicia got a small hospital started and she and Mr. and Mrs. Bracebridge continued to undertake the care of the soldiers' families throughout the campaign.

Meanwhile, although these extraneous duties took up a disproportionate amount of her time and energy, Florence always worked her hardest at the task for which she had primarily come to Scutari, the nursing of the soldiers. This was the part of the work she preferred; she was never so happy as in the wards and it was as a nurse that most people admired her. She had at last found her true vocation, and Parthe, in a rare flash of insight, wrote: 'In spite of it all have you not found your true home—the home of your spirit?' While the officials saw (and sometimes feared) the talented administrator, it was the sympathetic nurse that the soldiers loved and her kindness was what they most vividly remembered. The men idolized her and 'kissed her shadow' as she passed along the wards. For the work in the hospitals was growing daily, in spite of the fact that some of the Medical Officers still would not allow women nurses in their wards and it had to be one of Florence's strictest orders that they should work *only* where the doctors accepted them. Yet although they were excluded from some wards, on the night that the convoy arrived after the battle of Inkerman Florence could write with pardonable pride to a doctor friend: 'Between one and nine o'clock we had the mattresses stuffed, laid down —alas, only upon matting on the floor, the men washed and put to bed, and all their wounds dressed.' The wards were now full to overflowing; the palliasses had even to to be put in the corridors and almost up to the Sisters' Tower and on the 14th November Florence noted: 'We have *four miles* of beds and only eighteen inches apart.'

While during the day her nurses were in most parts of

the hospital, at night it was Florence herself who walked alone round these miles of beds carrying a lantern. She herself describes it to this same doctor: 'As I went my night-rounds among the newly wounded that first night, there was not one murmur, not one groan, the strictest discipline, the most absolute silence and quiet prevailed— only the steps of the Sentry—and I heard one man say, "I was dreaming of my friends at home," and another said, "I was thinking of them". These poor fellows bear pain and mutilation with an unshrinking heroism which is really superhuman.' This picture of the solitary figure going her rounds in the silent hospital captured the popular imagination and gave rise to her famous title, The Lady with a Lamp. Other countries caught the enthusiasm for her and the American poet, Longfellow, wrote a poem called Santa Filomena, which was soon as popular in England as in America. In this poem there are the much-quoted lines:

> Lo! in that house of misery
> A Lady with a Lamp I see
>   Pass through the glimmering gloom
>   And flit from room to room.
>
> And slow, as in a dream of bliss,
> The speechless sufferer turns to kiss
>   Her shadow, as it falls
>   Upon the darkening walls. . . .

Meanwhile the Lady herself was not concerned with poems but with the pressing problems which still continued to surround her. Those which most urgently demanded solution were three: the nurses, the officials and the religious antagonisms. With each of these she dealt in a different way. The most important one, and at the same time the most difficult to solve, was the problem of her nurses, for although some were doing excellent work, a great many were unsatisfactory and some utterly unreliable. Four of the St. John's House nurses, who might have been assumed to know what discipline meant, were unable to submit to it and had to be sent home. The behaviour of her nurses must have caused Florence the acutest anxiety for she knew that if they let her down the whole precarious experiment of employing women nurses in military hospitals might come to grief. She had also a strong feeling of responsibility towards Sidney Herbert, for if the venture failed he would incur much censure, and would moreover be as disappointed as Florence herself at this failure of a scheme that was so good in itself.

In the Nightingale Training School at St. Thomas's Hospital a large ledger is preserved which has almost a sad interest. It is the register kept by Florence Nightingale (though most of it is in Mrs. Bracebridge's handwriting) of all the nurses she had at Scutari, and against far too many names we find such entries as: 'dismissed for drunkenness' or 'proved utterly unreliable' or 'sent home for improper conduct'. In fact, of the thirty-eight she had brought out with her, Florence considered only sixteen really good nurses, but of those sixteen, six were so excellent that they were in a class by themselves. Among the nurses she most valued were Mrs. Roberts from St. Thomas's Hospital and Mrs. Drake from St. John's House; she also placed complete reliance on the Reverend Mother from Bermondsey and two of her Sisters. They remained until the end of the campaign and were some of Florence's most faithful supporters.

It would be interesting if we could know just how these nurses looked when they went about their work in the hospitals. We have few pictures of them, but the print on Plate 3 gives some idea of their appearance. One or two among them have also left graphic pen-pictures, and from these we can gather that the improvised uniform was, to put it mildly, not flattering! One nurse's protest against the cap evidently amused Florence so much that she recorded it in a letter home. 'I came out, Ma'am,' said Mrs. Lawfield, 'prepared to submit to everything, to be put upon in every way. But there are some things, Ma'am, one can't submit to. There is the Caps, Ma'am, that suits one face, and some that suits another.' In addition to this cap which aroused such resentment, they wore over their dark clothes a worsted jacket (Scutari is terribly cold in winter) and a grey tweed wrapper. Across their chest they had a large band, which one nurse called a 'frightful scarf', with the word 'Scutari' on it. It shows distinctly in the illustration. One or two of these bands have survived and may perhaps be said to be the forerunners of all women's military uniform. But Florence knew that the surroundings of her hospitals were very rough, as were also the manners of the camp followers, so these distinctive garments were really a protection, especially as it was quite a long walk from one hospital to another. She herself usually dressed very simply in black and wore a white cap.

With the officials Florence's relations gradually became somewhat easier, as she was always punctilious to observe every formality that was necessary and to conform abso-

lutely to military discipline. It was a more difficult matter
to enforce this conformity on her nurses, for many were
quite unused to discipline, but gradually her good example as well as her strict rules made themselves felt. For
Florence soon saw that, although they were slack and
sometimes deliberately obstructive, the officials themselves were often the victims of a bad system which they
were unable to alter. It was the multiplicity of departments at home, all of which had some share in the management of the Scutari hospitals and never agreed with one
another, that was the root cause of the muddle. This
divided control was, Florence felt, the death of all good
administration. With this was coupled a strong aversion
on the part of the officials to assume any responsibility; as
Florence herself indignantly said: 'It is a current joke here
to offer a prize to anyone ready to take responsibility.'
There was also complete indifference among some of the
medical officers to the prevailing conditions. One of
Florence's band accurately summed it up in the words:
'Generally speaking, the chief medical officers resolutely
closed their eyes to the great want in the hospitals of
every comfort for the patients: they would have said,
from time immemorial a prescribed course has been re-
sorted to in order to meet certain exigencies, and if it did
not meet them, it was *supposed* to do so; which was, they
persisted, as far as they were concerned, the same thing.'

The third difficulty with which Florence had to contend was that of religious antagonism. To us the bitterness
of feeling that she encountered seems almost inconceiv-
able. Many of her nurses were, as we saw, Roman
Catholic Sisters and some of them were accused of 'prose-
lytizing' among their non-Catholic patients. This accusa-

tion was countered by an assertion that some of the Pro-
testant nurses neglected their Roman Catholic patients.
All this sectarian animosity made the introduction of
female nurses into military hospitals an even more difficult task than it already was. It was incomprehensible to
Florence, who valued a nurse for the quality of her nursing and not for her religious tenets, that anyone could
waste time on those bickerings when so many important
things were still undone. She tried her utmost, however,
to distribute the Roman Catholics and the Protestants as
evenly as possible among the wards so as to silence further
criticism. She herself never descended into this arena of
sectarian intolerance and one clergyman said truly of her:
'She belongs to a sect which, unfortunately, is a very rare
one; the sect of the Good Samaritan.' What was to Florence much more important was the satisfaction of knowing that, since the nurses' arrival, the mortality among the
troops had dropped from forty-two per *hundred* to
twenty-two per *thousand* and that she could at last feel
that the invalids were also getting better nourishment.
Her diet kitchen, which had started on such a modest
scale, was really beginning to show results in the quicker
recovery of the patients.

After almost a month of unremitting and anxious work,
Florence could feel at the beginning of December 1854
that everything was really on the upward grade. What
was her consternation to hear that another party of about
fifty nurses and nuns was on its way out from England
and had left on the 2nd December under the leadership of
Miss Mary Stanley. This lady was the sister of Arthur
Stanley, the well-known Dean of Westminster, and she
and Florence had met in Rome in 1847; in fact, she and

Parthe had helped Florence only two months before in choosing her nurses. To say that Florence was appalled at the news would be to underrate her feelings. It was bad enough to have to absorb such a large party, for suitable accommodation in Scutari was all but unobtainable, but her consternation was complete when she learnt that the newcomers had received instructions to report not to her but to Dr. Cumming, the Inspector-General! Her states-manlike mind saw at once that this divided authority over the nurses put her in an impossible position and jeopard-ized the whole future of military nursing. She wrote very forcibly to Sidney Herbert, she even stated that she had been 'betrayed' and threatened to hand in her resignation and return home. Meanwhile something had to be done for Miss Stanley and her party, and, as the Principal Medi-cal Officer refused to have any more nurses in the Scutari hospitals, some were sent to the hospitals at Koulali, a vil-lage four miles farther north, and some direct to the Crimea. What made Florence so particularly bitter was that Mary Stanley, an old friend, seemed unable to under-stand the situation; if a 'friend', thought Florence, could act in this way, what would her 'enemies' do? Why Sid-ney Herbert had ever allowed these nurses to start and why they had received orders to report to the Inspector-General we shall never now know; perhaps it was merely the general confusion reigning at the War Office and the pressure of work with which he was overwhelmed and not 'a plot' as Florence furiously termed it. But the pres-ence of these women added greatly to her difficulties, for some of the Irish nuns proved difficult to handle and the lady-volunteers resented being made to conform to dis-cipline. They had no doubt formed a sentimental picture of attendance at the sick-bed and were not equal to the strain when confronted with the realities of work in a military hospital. A few of them appreciated the situation so little that they employed some of the nurses as their personal maids instead of in the hospital. In the end most of this new group of nurses, after considerable adjustment, were absorbed in the various hospitals, but between Florence and Mary Stanley the breach was never healed.

This unfortunate incident was barely closed when Christmas was upon Scutari and its hospitals. And the British soldier must celebrate Christmas in his own way whatever his surroundings! Florence, we may feel sure, entered heartily into their rejoicings. Queen Victoria had not forgotten her troops so far away. To Florence she sent a large consignment of comforts for her to distribute in the hospitals and each man had a gift from Her Majesty. The Queen followed up her gifts with a special message to her soldiers: 'I wish Miss Nightingale and the ladies would tell these poor noble wounded and sick men', wrote the Queen, 'that *no one* takes a warmer interest or feels *more* for their sufferings or admires their courage and heroism more than their Queen. Day and night she thinks of her beloved troops. So does the Prince.' This Royal message was read aloud by the Chaplain in the wards, and copies of it were posted in all the hospitals and the soldiers were much touched by the Queen's solicitude. Florence's nurses were also not forgotten, for Queen Victoria sent each one of them a scarf.

In February 1855, Florence was to have valuable assistance from an unexpected quarter. The War Office sent out a Commission to investigate the sanitary conditions at Scutari. It consisted of Dr. John Sutherland, Dr. Hector

Gavin and Mr. R. Rawlinson, a sanitary engineer. With Dr. Sutherland Florence formed a lifelong friendship. Here at last was a doctor who saw eye to eye with her on matters of hygiene. Dr. Sutherland unravelled the mystery of the awful smells that wafted through the wards of the Barrack Hospital and traced them to their origin. An open sewer ran right under the building, so the unhealthy state of the hospital needed no further explanation. Dr. Sutherland, who had been given full executive powers, quickly had this put right and effected many other sanitary improvements. The drastic reforms the Commissioners were empowered to carry out marked the turning point, in Florence's estimation, of the hygiene of the various hospitals.

CHAPTER FOUR

The Close of the Crimean War

By the spring of 1855, thanks to the work of this new Sanitary Commission as well as to that of the nurses, there had been a vast improvement in the condition of the hospitals at Scutari. Florence had been there about six months and felt that she could now safely be absent for a short time. The work had slackened considerably and there were at that moment only about eleven hundred patients in the Barrack Hospital. Her object was to go to the Crimea and judge for herself the condition of the hospitals there. She had already sent a few nurses to the Crimea under Miss Langston, the senior of the Sellon Sisters, and there were some of Miss Stanley's party in the General Hospital under Mother Bridgeman. This time she took with her one or two more nurses, including Mrs. Roberts of St. Thomas's Hospital. She was also accompanied by Mr. Bracebridge and Alexis Soyer, and, after an uncomfortable journey across the Black Sea on the *Robert Lowe*, they arrived at Balaclava on the 8th May 1855.

The difficulties and hardships that Florence had had to endure at Scutari paled before those that she encountered in the Crimea. To begin with, the distances between the hospitals were considerable. The island is very mountainous, and the so-called 'roads' were nothing but rough tracks impassable in bad weather. So she was forced to go from place to place on horseback or else, later, in a small carriage which had a hood to protect her from the rain or snow. This vehicle was not luxurious, but at any rate it was preferable to riding. It is now a treasured possession of the Nightingale School at St. Thomas's Hospital and, although badly damaged in the Battle of Britain, has since been restored.

But Florence's greatest difficulty was that her enemies among the officials in the Crimea took advantage of a technicality in order to humiliate her and make her work out there as difficult as possible. She had, probably by an oversight, been appointed by the War Office only 'Super-intendent of the Female Nursing Establishment in the English General Military Hospitals *in Turkey*', and those who resented her presence said that she had no jurisdiction over any nursing establishment in the *Crimea*! The Prin-cipal Medical Officer, Dr. John Hall, although outwardly correct, had always been prejudiced against her. The vin-dictiveness of those in authority even went so far that at one point they refused to give any rations to Florence and her nurses because they were 'not on the establishment', and on another occasion the party was kept waiting in the snow outside a hospital in order to gain admittance. She found also that although Mrs. Shaw Stewart at the Castle Hospital, Balaclava, was an exemplary Superintendent who loyally carried out her orders, the Irish Sisters under Mother Bridgeman at the General Hospital at Balaclava entirely repudiated her authority and stated that they would take orders from no one but Dr. Hall. But her adversaries had reckoned without the iron will of Flor-ence and her influence at home. She perfectly understood

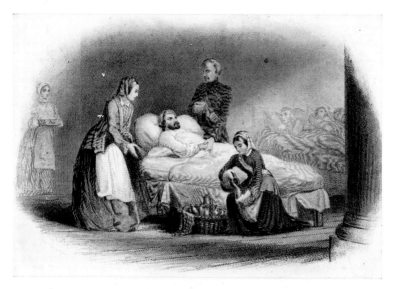

3. Florence Nightingale and her nurses at Scutari

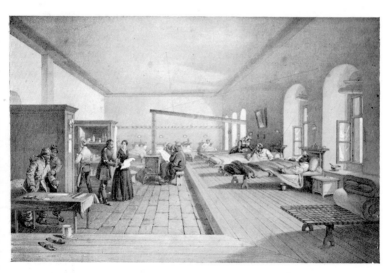

4. Florence Nightingale in the hospital at Scutari

the strength of her position and wrote to Sidney Herbert: 'There is not an official who would not burn me like Joan of Arc if he could, but they know that the War Office cannot turn me out because the country is with me.' So eventually rations were brought and doors were opened and Florence was able to go the rounds of the hospitals and establish nurses in those which still needed them. She was also able, with Soyer's help, to improve the cooking arrangements. Later, she helped to get institutes and reading-rooms started such as had been so valuable to the troops at Scutari. In *Soyer's Culinary Campaign*, the author has left us a vivid picture not only of the installation of these hospital kitchens but also of the many journeyings, especially those on horseback, of the Lady-in-Chief. He was much struck by her appearance and described her riding-habit as 'a very genteel Amazone'.

The mortality in the Crimean hospitals had been very high and the men suffered, as in the First World War, from exposure and frostbite as well as from wounds and disease. The commissariat also had broken down hopelessly, so hopelessly that the War Office had sent Sir John McNeill and Colonel A. Tulloch to inquire into the whole question and make a report. They arrived in the Crimea almost at the same time as Florence and both became in after years her close friends. Sir John and Colonel Tulloch found that the troops in the Crimea had not only suffered from inadequate and badly cooked food, but also that their uniforms were quite unsuited to withstand the rigours of the Russian winter. Their unnecessary sufferings goaded Florence to fury and she never rested until better provision had been made for them.

Whether it was due to the added difficulties and mental

stress of her work in the Crimea or whether it was the result of the greater physical hardships cannot now be known, but whatever was the cause Florence fell dangerously ill in the middle of May of what is always described as 'Crimean fever' and was perhaps typhus. For some days her condition was critical and she was nursed at the Castle Hospital with great devotion by Mrs. Roberts. During her time in hospital she was visited by Lord Raglan, the Commander-in-Chief. They never met again as he himself died only a month later. Everyone in England was appalled by the news of her illness and the soldiers in the Scutari hospitals are said to have wept, so completely had she won their love and devotion. This illness was not only serious to Florence at the time, but it had lifelong after effects on her health. When she was well enough to be moved, she went back to Scutari with Mrs. Bracebridge, who on hearing she was ill had followed her to the Crimea. For some time she convalesced, first at a house near the Barrack Hospital and afterwards at Therapia. Everyone urged her to take a longer rest, but she utterly refused to do so, saying: 'I am ready to stand out the war with any man.' By August she was back again in the full rush of work.

The news of Florence's illness and wonderful recovery spread like wildfire throughout England. She became the Popular Heroine and was even more fervently idolized. This moment, the autumn of 1855, marks the zenith of Florence's popularity; the adulation grew to almost ridiculous heights. Not only were countless little girls called Florence after the Heroine but her name was given to streets, to ships and even to race-horses! The poetasters were busy and popular ballads about her abounded. In every shop her admirers could buy a 'portrait', which bore only the remotest resemblance to the original. One enterprising shopkeeper in Derby even put one of these portraits on his paper bags and a few of these quaint relics are preserved in the Derby Museum to testify to the 'Nightingale Cult'. While her family perhaps found all this popular enthusiasm rather touching, Florence did not really relish it at all, as all through her long life she consistently mistrusted publicity. Yet in this instance publicity was useful as it brought about a valuable result.

Some among Florence's friends thought that the psychological moment had come to direct this enthusiasm into a practical channel. They knew that she would absolutely refuse any personal testimonial of the 'teapot and bracelet variety', as Parthe scornfully put it, but might welcome as a tribute to her national service some means of extending her work. So an influential committee was formed, with Sidney Herbert as an Honorary Secretary, and on 29th November 1855 a public meeting was held in London at which the Nightingale Fund was inaugurated. The chair was taken by the Duke of Cambridge, Queen Victoria's first-cousin, who was then the Commander-in-Chief, and the room was filled to overflowing with distinguished people. Sidney Herbert struck the right note when he said:

'Miss Nightingale looks to her reward from this country in having a fresh field for her labours, and the means of extending the good that she has already begun. A compliment cannot be paid dearer to her heart than in giving her work to do.'

The result of this and of many other meetings was that a sum of over £44,000 was collected. The donations that touched Florence most were those from the soldiers; they fully appreciated her services and out of the total they contributed the magnificent sum of £9,000. The later history of the Fund we must reserve for another chapter. Queen Victoria then sent Florence a personal token of her appreciation. The Prince Consort himself designed a jewel, which had the appearance of a badge rather than of an ordinary brooch, as it consisted of a St. George's Cross in red enamel and the Royal cypher surmounted by a crown in diamonds. With it came a personal letter from the Queen at Windsor.

'Dear Miss Nightingale,

'You are, I know, well aware of the high sense I entertain of the Christian devotion which you have displayed during this great and bloody war, and I need hardly repeat to you how warm my admiration is for your services, which are fully equal to those of my brave soldiers, whose sufferings you have had the *privilege* of alleviating in so merciful a manner. . . . It will be a very great satisfaction to me, when you return at last to these shores to make the acquaintance of one who has set so bright an example to our sex.'

Florence wore the jewel on special occasions to please the soldiers and it can now be seen among her other decorations in the United Service Museum in Whitehall.

When Florence was well enough to recommence her work she had the great joy of having Aunt Mai as her companion and helper. Mr. and Mrs. Bracebridge had gone home at the end of July 1855 not long after she had escorted Florence back from the Crimea at the beginning of her convalescence. Aunt Mai had arrived in September and found her dear niece deeper than ever in official work of which she could less well stand the fatigue as she had not fully shaken off the effects of her fever. The character of this work had indeed changed a good deal since that of a year before. Florence was no longer able to do so much actual nursing, for her office work had so vastly increased. She who so loved the actual attendance at the bedside was forced to spend most of her time in administrative duties such as interviewing officials, or writing letters or reports or keeping accounts. She was able to do this more easily than in the previous year as she had now a larger staff of nurses; by the end of the war there were one hundred and twenty-five under her control.

To another enterprise for the soldiers in which she felt great interest Florence could also now give more of her attention. Ever since her arrival at Scutari she had been much worried by the drunkenness among the troops and sought to diminish it by providing counter-attractions to the 'dram shop'. There was nowhere, she saw, for the men to go, whether they were convalescent or merely off duty, to spend their time in pleasant surroundings. This situation called for immediate action. Characteristically, Florence did not wait for government support to start this new experiment, but opened a reading-room near the Barrack Hospital from private funds and furnished it with books, magazines and games. In providing a place for the men to spend their leisure she was as much a pioneer as in many other matters. The military hierarchy looked rather askance at the whole proceeding and were more often apathetic than co-operative. She was 'spoiling the brutes', they said, and doing something that was quite unnecessary. But soon the original reading-room was followed by

the 'Inkerman Café', a much larger building near the Bosphorus, and this venture had Royal support. Queen Victoria, when she heard about the Café, sent a picture for
its adornment and many of Florence's friends in England
despatched books and other supplies. Florence quickly
followed this up by getting classes established and two
schoolmasters were sent out from England. Soon after
this a system of manual training was begun and work-
shops were opened. Sir Henry Storks, who was now the
Commandant at Scutari, gave his unfailing support. He
bought, on behalf of the government, a large building
near the Barrack Hospital in which reading-rooms as well
as class-rooms could be housed, and soon similar institutes
were started in the Crimea.

The soldiers were further aided by Florence to help
their families at home. She started an arrangement by
which they could voluntarily remit part of their pay to
their families, since the present system of separation allow-
ances had not then been inaugurated. Here again the
gloomy prophecies of the officers were not at all fulfilled.
'The British soldier', said the pessimists, 'is not a remitting
animal,' but they were wrong. Florence remitted home
about £1,000 each month which was all, as she said,
money 'rescued' from expenditure on drink. This was yet
another instance of how she anticipated official action by
many years.

While she was so much concerned for the moral welfare of the troops, Florence did not forget the needs of the
doctors. Having found that the medical officers had no
place where they could do any investigations or any
scientific work, she quickly procured a house in Scutari at
her own expense, and arranged that it should be equipped

with the necessary scientific instruments. This small and humble beginning was the nucleus of the future Army Medical School.

During the last six months of her stay in the East, Florence divided her time between Scutari and the Crimea. She paid in all two visits to the Crimea after her illness, one in the late autumn of 1855 and another in the early part of 1856. Peace was declared in March 1856, but the hospitals did not close until the summer and she finally left Turkey late in July. An offer of a man-of-war to take her back to England was refused and, travelling as Miss Smith, she returned with Aunt Mai in August, and slipped back unnoticed to Lea Hurst.

CHAPTER FIVE

War's Aftermath—Florence Nightingale's Work for the Royal Commissions

It was such a treat to get their dear daughter back safe and sound, that her parents probably did not fully realize that the Florence who turned up unannounced that August evening at Lea Hurst was a very different person from the woman who had gone to the East two years before. To begin with, she looked different. Even we, who have only a few photographs to guide us, can see that the face is thinner, the expression more serious and in some cases almost severe. Her hair had not yet grown since her illness of the year before, a fact that must have rather horrified her relations, since it was unheard-of at that time for a woman ever to have it cut short. In conformity with the prevailing fashion, Florence wore a lace cap so that her hair does not show very much, but the later photographs, when her hair had grown again, are far more pleasing. What her family realized still less was that the change her personality had undergone was even greater than that of her appearance. She had left for Turkey a woman of talents and ability but with this ability as yet untested; she returned a mature and resolute reformer, determined at all costs to capitalize the prestige which her unique position as 'Heroine of the Crimea' had given her, for the advancement of her cause. For her own glorification she cared not at all since she had what someone has called 'a conspicuous absence of self-advertisement'. As she had no position to win or lose, she was completely disinterested and she was never a party politician. While the world regarded her achievement in the Crimea as the culmination of her work, she saw it merely as an incident which, by giving her unique experience, had made her peculiarly fitted for further endeavour; indeed it was to her (to quote a biographer) 'not a climax but an episode'. This is very important to remember in considering the rest of her career.

After their delighted welcome was over, we can guess that the first thing her relations begged Florence to do was to have a good rest. She had been almost two years away from home and, except for those anxious days when she had lain so ill with fever in the Crimea, had never had even a day's holiday. They would have known also, even without Aunt Mai's letters from Scutari, that their Florence had worked with a concentration and a ceaseless energy that would have worn out even the strongest. But whenever anyone suggested how necessary it was to give her tired body and equally tired mind complete relaxation, Florence would not listen and felt that she must know best. She would not pay any attention to Sidney Herbert or even to a physician, her dear Dr. Sutherland, who urged her, a little later on, to have at least one week's holiday if she would take no more! As events were to prove, her friends were right and she was most certainly wrong, for she did need the rest they all urged her to take, and paid for her refusal to follow their advice by a lifetime of ill health. She had probably got to the nervous condition in which she *could not* stop working and was suffering from what we should now call a complete nervous breakdown; her heart also had been affected by the strain of her severe illness. It is possible that doctors did not then so thoroughly understand this type of complaint as they would now, and she was, admittedly, a particularly difficult patient. In any event many years passed before she regained even moderately good health and she was often so severely prostrated with illness that the doctors despaired of her life.

Where others had sacrificed their lives in the Crimean campaign, Florence Nightingale made an almost equally complete sacrifice of her health. It was only her indomitable will and exceptional mental powers that enabled her to keep going at all. What drove her on was the conviction, which we should all have had in her position, that if she did not continue her work for the soldiers *at once* it would come to nothing. The general public had perhaps already forgotten their sufferings, or if they had not actually forgotten the Crimean tragedy, Florence knew that they would be at best quite apathetic about any suggestions to prevent such disasters from happening again. Florence was a believer, if anyone ever was, in striking while the iron was hot; she understood human nature so well that she knew that delay would be fatal. She had another deeper, and to her more sacred, reason for continuing to work for 'her children', as she often called the soldiers. It was, she felt, a solemn duty laid upon her. In a private note-book she wrote: 'I stand at the altar of the murdered men and while I live I fight their cause.' By this forcible expression we see that she considered that the troops in the late war had been 'murdered' not so much by the enemy's rifles as by the criminal mismanagement of responsible people in England and the callous neglect of those in authority on the spot. Florence felt that her life was dedicated to avenge these 'murders' by ensuring that, as far as was humanly possible, the lessons of the war should not be neglected.

Her feelings on this subject were particularly bitter and in another place she wrote: 'No one can feel for the Army as I do. These people who talk to us have all fed their children on the fat of the land and dressed them in velvet and silk, while we have been away. I have had to see my children dressed in a dirty blanket and an old pair of regimental trousers and to see them fed on raw salt meat, and nine thousand of my children are lying, from causes which might have been prevented, in their forgotten graves. But I can never forget.' She must even have spent some part of this breathing space at Lea Hurst in planning out the course of action for her campaign, for by November she was back in London and immersed in official business.

Before returning to London, however, Florence had the chance of pleading the cause of 'her children' before her Sovereign. She regarded this as an opportunity too important to be missed. In August 1856 she went up to Scotland to stay with her friend, Sir James Clark, Queen Victoria's physician, at Birk Hall, near Ballater. Birk Hall was very near Balmoral, and on 19th September Florence was commanded to come to the Castle. The visit was of an entirely unofficial nature, but Florence did not waste her time, for the Prince Consort commented afterwards: 'She put before us all the defects of our present military hospital system; and the reforms that are needed. We are much pleased with her; she is extremely modest.' Queen Victoria was so much struck with Florence that a week

later she came over to Birk Hall to see her and have another private talk, and in a letter afterwards to the Duke
of Cambridge made the classic remark: 'We . . . are very
much struck . . . by her wonderful, clear and comprehen-
sive head. I wish we had her at the War Office.' A week
or so later Lord Panmure, the Secretary for War, was at
Balmoral and Florence was advised by the Queen to stay
and see him. They had an interview in which Florence
made preliminary suggestions about some of the reforms
which she felt to be necessary. He also seemed impressed
by her knowledge, but would not commit himself. So
with the approval of the Queen and the friendly interest
of the Queen's Minister, Florence returned to London to
her great task.

After her return from the Crimea, Florence never again
went home to her family as a permanent member of the
household. She had won her independence at a great price
and this freedom she meant to keep. From that moment
she put her work first. The nature of this work demanded
that she should be either in London or very near it, but
for the first few years after 1856 she seems to have shrunk
from the burden of owning and running a house, and was
for a time very restless. She often stayed in a hotel, at
other times we find her in lodgings at Hampstead or at
Highgate, and she sometimes took furnished houses in
London. Occasionally she went to Malvern for a change.
Her father's generous money provision enabled her to be
financially independent and finally to have a comfortable
house run by a competent staff. But whether she was living in a hotel, or later, when she eventually established
herself at 10 South Street, Mayfair, she never materially
altered the way of life which, early in her career, she de-

cided to adopt. Afterwards it became a matter of habit and she maintained it unchanged right up to the end. She chose to live alone, because she felt that in this way she would be free from the interruptions inevitable in ordinary family life and be able to devote herself exclusively to her work. Of what we now regard as normal social intercourse she had none; she did not often see people except on business and never received casual callers, or went out to pay even informal visits to close friends.

Although, when she finally owned a house, she was generous in her hospitality and frequently entertained people, especially nurses, in the years to come, these guests did not necessarily see their hostess even though they might be staying under her roof. This voluntarily assumed isolation was at first dictated by the poor state of her health. What strength she had, Florence felt, must be wholly devoted to the tasks that she had to do, and not be frittered away on social engagements. She considered that now even family ties must take a second place. 'Indeed we know', wrote a friend to her father, 'how hard it is for you to hear nothing of her, but no one can know anything now that the isolation of work has set in.' Later, when the sphere of her activities widened and there were even more calls upon her time and limited strength, she found that her self-imposed seclusion proved very convenient as it guarded her from bores, from uncongenial people and from those whose desire to see her was prompted merely by idle curiosity and not by genuine interest in her work. She considered that she had no time to waste on such visitors and against them her door was resolutely barred. No one saw her without an appointment and even when one of her real friends, such as Dr.

Sutherland, was actually in the house working with her their means of communication might be sometimes by notes which passed between them, Dr. Sutherland sitting downstairs while she remained upstairs.

Yet she was always approachable to her younger relations in whom she inspired great devotion. One of her cousins says: 'Though of course as a child I knew very little of Miss Nightingale's work, I was aware that she was very busy. We did not drop in casually to see her, our visits were nearly always made by appointment so as not to clash with her other engagements. . . . She always gave one the warmest of welcomes, talked and listened with her fullest attention, and was constantly wanting to do some kindness—to think of a suitable birthday present or the like.'

Although this way of ordering her life enabled Florence to do an amount of work, unaided by any regular secretary, that sometimes seems incredible, yet it tended to cut her off from a great number of people and prevented her from having a balanced outlook. Since her visitors came only one at a time she was deprived of ordinary friendly intercourse, nor did she ever have the advantage or the interest of hearing two people discussing some point in her presence, or of obtaining more than one opinion at a time on any subject. Her life was, in fact, so restricted that it is yet another tribute to her remarkable intellect and to her power of keeping abreast of what was going on, that she should not have been more remote from the life around her. She spent a great part of her time in her own room, sometimes entirely confined to her bed, and it was in this room that the interviews took place.

Later on she occasionally made a break in her routine

and went to stay at Lea Hurst or at Embley Park, sometimes for several months at a time, especially after her
father's death in 1874. After her sister married Sir Harry
Verney in 1858, she was also a frequent visitor to their
home, Claydon, in Buckinghamshire. But the only house
that was really her own was in London and she lived
in 10 South Street, Mayfair (now demolished), from
1865 until her death in 1910.

When Florence came back from Turkey in 1856, most
people knew that she had withdrawn from the public eye
and imagined, no doubt, that she was leading a life of ease
in this retirement. As she always mistrusted publicity she
was perhaps glad to let everyone think this. Little did any
except her circle of intimate friends know that she had
indeed 'retired', not to a life of leisure but to years of
gruelling and exacting labour. Of this labour a close
friend wrote: 'The Nation is grateful to you for what you
did at Scutari, but all that it was possible for you to do
there was a trifle compared with the good you are doing
now.'

Only a few months had passed since her return from
the East before Florence was ensconced in London and
deeply engaged in official work of the most important
kind. It is very difficult for any of us at the present day
fully to appreciate the curious way in which she was
forced to carry out this work. To understand it we must
consider for a moment what had happened since the close
of the Crimean War. A Royal Commission had been
suggested to inquire into the causes of the Crimean
muddle. Such a Commission, in 1856 as at the present
time, consisted of disinterested people chosen by the
Crown to make an inquiry into any special subject. To-

day Florence would unquestionably have been made a member of the Commission and have taken an active share in this national work. In the 1850's, however, the appointment of a woman was unheard of, nor did she even give evidence in person before the Commissioners. Yet they did not wish to forgo the benefit of her expert advice, so they compromised by submitting some written questions to her to which she likewise answered in writing. During the whole time that the Commission was at work Florence was forced to occupy what seems to us a perfectly impossible position, a position we should consider most hampering and unsatisfactory. She was the 'Power behind the Throne' or, in other words, the person behind the scenes who really got things done but through the medium of other people. In this case the 'other people' were Florence's good friends, Sidney Herbert and Dr. Sutherland. In order to be near at hand she took rooms in the Burlington Hotel which no longer exists. It was very convenient, as it was in Old Burlington Street, just behind Burlington House in Piccadilly. There these three people could be found at work almost every day and the Hotel was sometimes nicknamed the 'Little War Office'. Queen Victoria had offered Florence Nightingale rooms in Kensington Palace, but she had declined them as being too far away. This may seem odd to us, as we should not now consider Kensington Palace off the beaten track, but then there was no Underground and Florence's busy colleagues would have had to come the three miles from Whitehall by a slow horse carriage or an even slower horse bus.

The Commission was, to Florence's impatient way of thinking, very slow in getting to business. Lord Panmure

5. Florence Nightingale in 1906

had approved it in principle at the end of 1856, but it was not officially appointed until May 1857. Its Report was not finished until August of that same year and was published in February 1858. At every stage in the writing of this Report, Florence did most of the work, for she had the first-hand knowledge, which Sidney Herbert lacked, of everything that had happened in the Crimean hospitals. It is no exaggeration to say that it could never have been written without her. To us, nearly a hundred years after, this Report seems remote from reality, but to Florence every word was of the utmost importance, for she and her colleagues knew that it was only by this means that the conscience of the general public could be aroused. They also hoped, of course, that Parliament would pass legislation which would benefit the soldier of the future. Florence wrote, or helped to write, a great part of the whole Report, but she did not of course sign any part of it except one section entitled 'Questions and Answers'. These were the questions which the Commissioners had sent her, together with her replies. The 'Questions' covered every aspect of hospital management and nursing, and in her 'Answers' she was able to embody her criticisms of army methods and outline the means she thought should be taken to improve them.

Yet Florence's work for this Commission, that she felt to be so important, did not end with her share in the Report. At the request of Lord Panmure, she agreed to embark upon an even bigger undertaking, namely the preparation of a further report of her own on the administration of the Crimean hospitals. This entailed the writing of a very long book with the awkward title of *Notes on Matters affecting the Health, Efficiency and Hospital Adminis-*

tration of the British Army. In it she was able to go into every question affecting the medical services in even greater detail than had been possible in the actual Report and be even more unsparing in her criticisms. To this remarkable book we shall refer later.

What gave Florence even more to do in the years from 1858 to 1861 were the four Sub-Commissions, as they were called, which were the outcome of the main Commission. In 1859 Sidney Herbert had become Secretary of State for War and he was the Chairman of each of these four Sub-Commissions which were all concerned with matters connected with the welfare of the Army. Details about these Sub-Commissions would be out of place here, but, in brief, the first two dealt respectively with the improvement of barracks and with establishing a military Statistical Department. The third Sub-Commission went into the question of founding an Army Medical School, while the business of the fourth was the reform of hospital regulations and of various other matters connected with the Army Medical Department. They were all, as we can see, concerned with subjects on which Florence felt particularly strongly; they were also constructive and she always looked to tangible results and regarded mere theorizing as great waste of time.

The Sub-Commission on the barracks Florence felt to be of special importance. From personal experience she knew how fatal insanitary surroundings were to the soldiers—or as she tersely put it: 'Our soldiers enlist to death in the barracks.' Florence must have staggered her colleagues by producing, in her characteristic way, statistics which showed that the death-rate was higher among healthy young soldiers in barracks than among the civilian population. This was indeed a bombshell. She proved her points by giving actual figures, and also by drawing diagrams, or graphs, to make the statistics easier to understand. We are so familiar to-day with every kind of graph, or visual presentation of facts, that it is difficult to realize that Florence was a pioneer in their use. This high mortality, she went on to show, was entirely due to preventable causes. The most important of these was that the barracks were badly built and badly ventilated (Florence always preached the Gospel of Fresh Air!) and that the food provided for the men was inadequate, as well as being poorly chosen and even more poorly cooked. Probably every man in the Army to-day owes something to what Florence then did and she was rightly called the 'Providence of the Army'. In this instance she had the happiness of seeing a great improvement in barrack construction during her lifetime.

The next two Sub-Commissions were likewise on subjects very dear to her. She had always been profoundly interested in statistics and had already shown, during the war, her keenness in regard to the creation of an Army Medical School. She was convinced that the training of doctors for the Army ought to be improved and used all the weight of her influence to forward the founding of this School. Florence had had more practical experience of the actual work of Army surgeons on active service than many officials in the War Office. While she admitted that the efficiency of the doctors varied considerably, she felt that, without exception, they had all been handicapped by inadequate training. The results of the labours of this particular Sub-Commission can be seen to-day in the Army Medical School at Millbank. To the fourth of the Sub-

Commissions, which was concerned with a variety of questions about the Army Medical Department and Army hospitals, she likewise gave the benefit of her expert knowledge when it was needed.

But the government work on which Florence was engaged was soon to receive a death-blow. Sidney Herbert's health began to give way at the beginning of 1860 and by the end of that year he was in a critical condition. In January 1861 he was created Lord Herbert of Lea, but he did not live long to play his part in the House of Lords as he died on 2nd August. With him died many of the projects for Army reform and reconstruction on which he and Florence and their colleagues had been working.

The death of Lord Herbert was an important milestone in Florence's career, for it marked the end of the first period of her work. She was overwhelmed with sorrow and her grief for Lady Herbert was very great. But in addition to her sense of personal loss was her foreboding that, without Lord Herbert's support, the measures on which they had both laboured for five long years would be put aside. It was the loyal colleague that she mourned as well as the true friend. He seems to have felt the same anxiety about the future, for it is told that as he was dying he murmured: 'Poor Florence, poor Florence; our joint work left unfinished.' From that moment she never found anyone with whom she so much enjoyed working; he was the ideal colleague and his loss was irreparable. Not even her close friend, Dr. Sutherland, quite filled the blank in her life and work left by Sidney Herbert.

At first Florence seems to have been so utterly prostrated by grief that her powers of concentration were almost paralysed. The future looked so bleak that she was nearly in despair. But her strength of character soon asserted itself and she forced herself to toil with even greater intensity for the causes that they had both had so much at heart. She wished to make her work a tribute to Sidney Herbert and an abiding monument to all that he had done for the Army. The close of this same year, 1861, brought Florence a fresh bereavement. In November, Arthur Hugh Clough, the poet, died in Italy. His wife was her first-cousin and he had been for some years Florence's devoted helper both in her work for the government and for nursing. It seemed as though this added blow would quite overwhelm her, yet when the first bitter sorrow had passed away she solaced her grief by working harder than ever.

CHAPTER SIX

The Founding of the Nightingale School and Florence Nightingale's Other Work for Nursing

By about the beginning of 1859 Florence had more or less finished this intensive and exacting work for the Royal Commissions and felt able to give her time to other interests. She had not forgotten the large sum of money that had been subscribed in 1855 to found 'an English Kaiserswerth', or something similar, but even from Scutari she had warned the subscribers that she could give no precise date as to when the money could be utilized and the project become a practical reality. The moment had now arrived, she felt, when she might take definite steps. There was also a good deal of writing, other than that in government publications, that she wanted to do. Two books of hers belong to this year, 1859, namely *Notes on Nursing* and *Notes on Hospitals*. This first book, *Notes on Nursing*, is the best-known thing she ever wrote, and it had an immense success.

This success may perhaps have consoled Florence in some measure for the deep disappointment in store for her in this same year. When her friends and supporters had held that historic meeting to initiate the Nightingale Fund they had unquestionably assumed that Florence herself would be the head of whatever school, or other establishment, she might start for the training of nurses. Florence had doubtless thought the same herself when, at Scutari, she had originally heard of the Fund, and even for some time afterwards pictured herself as a Superintendent. But it was gradually borne in upon her that her health was not equal to undertaking such a task. She may several times have felt that her condition might yet improve and that she would still do what she had so ardently hoped to accomplish, but by 1859 the sad truth had reluctantly to be acknowledged that she was not in a fit state to begin it. We can never know how great her disappointment was, for it seems to have been too deep a sorrow to mention even to her dearest friends. It was the dream of a lifetime shattered. But still, being Florence Nightingale, she did not allow personal regrets to stand in the way of carrying out her plan for initiating what she felt to be so essential. As she now saw that she must accomplish this plan of training nurses through other people she started making definite arrangements. A small sub-committee of the Nightingale Fund was formed and made inquiries at several hospitals in London. Florence was never well enough to go with them, but she took careful notes of all they told her. In the end the choice fell on St. Thomas's Hospital, and it was there that the Nightingale School was established the next year.

In 1860 St. Thomas's was not housed in the large building whose long row of pavilions opposite the Houses of Parliament are so familiar to every Londoner. The hospital was still at that date in Southwark, near Southwark Cathedral, where it had occupied since the twelfth century a site now covered by London Bridge Station. This area had already been sold to the South Eastern Railway Company and it was only a matter of time before the hospital would have to be rebuilt in a different place. There were several reasons why St. Thomas's appeared particularly suitable to Florence and her advisers, but the main points in its favour were three. The first was the most important, in Florence's view at least, and that was that the Matron, Mrs. Wardroper, was a woman after her own heart. Florence had already been struck, when she had been recruiting her nurses for the East, by the Matron's remarkable personality. Mrs. Wardroper was an educated woman, far superior to most matrons of her day, and she had already taken steps to try to improve the quality of the nurses on the St. Thomas's staff. In all her writings Florence constantly reiterated her belief that a good matron is the key to a successful training school, so she felt that in Mrs. Wardroper's capable hands this unprecedented experiment might have a fair chance of success. The second reason was that the Resident Medical Officer, Mr. Whitfield, was sympathetic with the scheme and promised it his support. Florence had already had dealings with Mr. Whitfield and had written from Scutari to her friend, Dr. Bowman: 'If you ever see Mr. Whitfield, will you tell him that the nurse he sent me, Mrs. Roberts, is worth her weight in gold.' The third reason may seem to us rather less important and this was the fact that the hospital was soon to have new buildings. But since Florence had very decided views about the correct construction of hospitals and of nurses' homes, she felt that here she would have some chance of ensuring that the hospital was built as she wanted it. When the new St. Thomas's that we know was opened by Queen Victoria in June 1871, it was constructed on the 'pavilion' plan which Florence regarded as the healthiest and the new Nightingale Home, which was to take the place of the original home in the old hospital at Southwark, had been incorporated as an integral part of the whole design. It remained the home of the Nightingale probationers until it was extensively damaged by an air raid in 1941.

When St. Thomas's had been chosen, the next thing to do was to make the final business arrangements with the governors of the hospital and then to secure some suitable women to undergo training. Florence thought that at first it would be better if the number of pupils was small, so in the end, on 9th July 1860, fifteen probationers entered the Nightingale School for training, and this day may really be said to be the birthday of modern nursing.

About these original fifteen women very little is known, but we can imagine that they gave Florence great satisfaction and that she felt pardonable pride in the fact that she had actually launched her revolutionary venture—for such everyone considered it. It is interesting to realize, now that we regard trained nurses as a commonplace and would be surprised if they did not exist, that the whole idea of giving nurses *a training* was regarded as rather unnecessary. The general public was by no means enthusiastic. Among some people there was complete indifference, or polite scepticism, while certain doctors were definitely opposed to the whole idea as being 'new-fangled' and fanciful. They felt that the old-fashioned nurses 'did very well as they were', and one surgeon of St. Thomas's itself, who was at one time President of the Royal College of Surgeons, said: 'As regards the nurses or ward-maids, these are in much the same position as housemaids, and require little teaching beyond that of poultice-making.'

Although we may not know much about these first 'Nightingales', yet we possess many details about the system of training which Florence evolved and the terms under which the hospital accepted them. The probationers were to be admitted for a year's training, the hospital giving them the opportunity for gaining practical experience in the wards and the Nightingale Fund paying their salary and maintenance. Florence also arranged that their theoretical instruction was to be undertaken by the doctors who were to give them lectures in anatomy and other subjects. If, after this year of training, a nurse proved suitable, she sometimes stayed on for a second year at St. Thomas's to acquire the further experience that should fit her to go out in her turn as a Superintendent and so bring the benefits of trained nursing to other hospitals.

Florence also laid great stress in her system of training on suitable surroundings for her nurses, and she considered that the physical well-being and high moral tone imparted by a proper 'home' under a special 'Home Sister' were second only in importance to a good matron. This, again, was an entirely new idea to hospital authorities and the 'Nightingale Home' was almost, in the view of some critics, as 'newfangled' as the 'Nightingale Nurse' herself. Since nurses' homes are quite as usual now as the nurses who live in them, this attitude is also one that we find difficult to understand. The governors of St. Thomas's allotted the top floor of one wing in the old hospital to be fitted up as the Nightingale Nurses' Home. Each probationer had a bedroom of her own and a cheerful communal sitting-room was provided. We can imagine with what loving care Florence superintended the arrangement of this home and what pains she took to have the sitting-room pleasantly furnished and provided with books and flowers. From the moment that the Nightingale School was launched Florence took the keenest possible interest in every pupil. It was very much *her* school, for although Mrs. Wardroper was responsible for the day-to-day management of the nurses' work, yet every detail of the training was thought out by Florence and planned in consultation with her. The collaboration of these two remarkable women, each with a very strong personality, over a period of some twenty-five years, is an almost unique example of successful co-operation.

Some of the rules for the Nightingale nurses, which Florence herself drew up in collaboration with Mrs. Wardroper, appear to us very strict, indeed harsh. It seems remarkable that they needed to be so strict, since the probationers were much older than they are now. Florence did not wish any candidate to be admitted under the age of twenty-five and it was not uncommon for women to begin their training in their early thirties. But one should not forget that, even though the pupils were older, the whole undertaking was an *experiment*, that 'trained' nurses were not accepted as they are nowadays and that one slip, or one lapse from correct behaviour, on the part of a pupil might have wrecked the whole scheme. We should also bear in mind that the average daughter from the average Victorian family had been accustomed to much stricter discipline in her own home than is usual at the present time, and may not have considered the hospital discipline as severe as we do. The regulations regarding the probationers' appearance were equally rigid and seem to us quaint; when off duty they were to wear bonnets, not hats, and these bonnets were not to be trimmed with flowers, nor were they allowed to arrange their hair in any but the plainest fashion. Furthermore, they were permitted to go outside the hospital only in groups of two or three together. We should remember, however, that Southwark was a rough neighbourhood in those days, as we can see from many of Dickens's novels, and Florence did not wish her 'new' nurses to give anyone the slightest cause for criticism.

But by far the most original feature of Florence's scheme of nurse-training, beside which these rules of deportment and dress are insignificant, was the unique system of reports on each nurse. By these she aimed at following closely the career of each individual pupil. The system, to which Florence had given years of thought, was utterly characteristic of her passion for accuracy and thoroughness and could have been evolved by no one else. Florence was first and foremost an educationalist, and, by keeping this close watch on their progress, she hoped to ensure that each nurse who left the Nightingale School should not only have had her character developed but should also have received an extremely thorough professional training. To achieve this result Florence drew up an elaborate 'Monthly Sheet of Personal Character and Achievements of each nurse', which the matron had to fill in under many headings. There was a Moral Record and a Technical Record, both with many subdivisions, and against each item on the sheet the matron had to mark 'Excellent', 'Good', 'Moderate' or 'Imperfect', according to the nurse's achievements. Only a perfectionist like Florence could have thought out anything so detailed and, as one of her biographers expresses it: 'No public school, university, or other institution ever had so elaborate and exhaustive a system of marks.'

At about the same time as the school at St. Thomas's was started, Florence decided to allocate part of the Nightingale Fund to the training of midwives. She felt that it was very important to improve their professional education and status as well as that of nurses and she arranged to send a few pupils to work at King's College Hospital. But the experiment, which started so well and appeared to be so promising, had to be terminated only six years later owing to an outbreak of puerperal fever in the maternity wards, and Florence did not subsequently start a similar undertaking in any other hospital.

The light of the young Nightingale School at St. Thomas's was not permitted to remain long hidden under a bushel. Even by January 1861 Mrs. Wardroper began to have applications for her nurses and in 1862 Florence was consulted by Mr. William Rathbone, a public-spirited and philanthropic citizen of Liverpool, who became afterwards one of her closest friends. Mr. Rathbone wished to inaugurate a system by which the poor could be nursed by trained nurses in their own homes as well as in hospital. It must have been a gratification to Florence to think that so soon she should receive an appeal for help in spreading the training of nurses, and the subject of nursing in the home, as well as in the hospital, was always particularly near her heart. But she was not able to do exactly what Mr. Rathbone wished. He asked her to supply him with some trained nurses to begin a new school of nursing, but she had to reply that she had none that she could spare and advised him to train his own.

Consequently, in 1862, a training school was built and equipped by Mr. Rathbone at the Royal Infirmary, Liverpool, and the nurses were there prepared for nursing in both hospital and home. Liverpool was thus the first training school outside London to be run on 'Nightingale' principles and its first Superintendent was Miss Merry-weather, who received a short training at St. Thomas's. Florence always remained in particularly close touch with this Liverpool school.

A year or so later, when the Nightingale School had been running for four years, another call came from Liverpool, and Mr. Rathbone, that was even more of a challenge to existing nursing systems. Mr. Rathbone had been horrified at the state of the so-called nursing in the Workhouse Infirmaries and was resolved to try the bold experiment of introducing trained nurses. So he did again what everyone soon learnt to do, he went to Florence and propounded this new scheme. A hundred years ago the workhouses admitted all destitute persons who were able-bodied and they often had an Infirmary attached to ac-commodate the sick. Mr. Rathbone could have told Florence, only that she knew already, the horrible condi-tions then prevailing in these Infirmaries where there was no separation between pauper children, inmates who were really ill and inmates who were insane. Charles Dickens in 1838 had put the pauper child of the workhouse in the limelight by writing *Oliver Twist*, but even he had not told the whole story. The only 'nurses' for the sick were those among the pauper women who were slightly less drunken or slightly less decrepit than the rest. Mr. Rath-bone had chosen a subject that also appealed strongly to Florence and she threw herself into it with her accustomed vigour. In 1864 she chose Agnes Jones, one of the best pupils in the Nightingale School, for this pioneer undertaking. Agnes Jones, like Florence herself, had gone to Kaiserswerth and then had had a year in the Nightingale School and some subsequent hospital experience. She was a refined and gifted young woman with great qualities of leadership. After prolonged preliminary negotiations she went to the Brownlow Hill Infirmary, Liverpool, on 16th May 1865 with twelve other Nightingale nurses, their salaries being paid by Mr. Rathbone. Within a year she and these nurses had managed to make improvements that seem almost miraculous and the success of the experiment was assured. But Agnes Jones could not avoid the infection rampant in her hospital and she died of typhus in February 1868, a true martyr to the cause. Her death was a great blow to Florence and in after years she always regarded her as the ideal of what a Nightingale nurse should be.

Agnes Jones, however, had not died in vain, for the principle of trained nursing in workhouses was firmly established in Liverpool and its example was soon to be followed in London and other cities. Florence worked particularly hard for this cause; in fact, it occupied a great part of her time in the years immediately prior to 1867. In that year, after a long political campaign into which she entered with zest, the Metropolitan Poor Act was passed to reform the Workhouse Infirmaries of London. The Act insisted, among other changes, on what Florence felt to be so important, namely the introduction of trained nursing. She contributed a masterly study to the massive government report on the subject and very shortly after sent a 'Nightingale' to begin, in 1869, a training school in the new infirmary at Highgate. Florence lived to see the time when, in 1897, pauper nurses were forbidden to be employed in any Infirmary, in any part of England, and the seal seemed set on this part of her all-embracing work for nursing.

Ever since Mr. Rathbone had shown the way in Liverpool, Florence determined to forward a branch of nursing that had a peculiar appeal for her, namely District (or Visiting) Nursing. She felt strongly that trained nursing had done only half its job if patients outside hospital were not as well nursed as those within. As she said: 'Never think that you have done anything effectual in nursing in London till you nurse, not only the sick poor in workhouses, but those at home.' So she threw herself heart and soul into the founding in 1875 of the Metropolitan and National Nursing Association and chose the Nightingale nurse, Miss F. Lees (afterwards Mrs. Dacre Craven), who was its first director. She followed this up by writing a long letter to *The Times* in the next year pleading the cause of District Nursing, and the prestige of her name carried great weight in the appeal. With her usual prophetic insight she wrote of District Nursing: 'Twenty years ago it was a paradox, but twenty years hence will be a common-place', and she lived to see her prophecy fulfilled. Some years later, in 1887, when she was mature in experience, she gave her support and much valuable advice to the newly started Queen's Institute of District Nursing, founded in honour of Queen Victoria's Jubilee.

Meanwhile, Florence had never forgotten her primary interest, Army nursing. Her former Crimean colleague, Mrs. Shaw Stewart, was chosen in 1861 to be Superintendent of the nursing staff of the military hospital, called the Herbert Hospital, at Woolwich, and afterwards of the new Army hospital at Netley. From that moment Florence followed the career of every Army nurse with great interest and was constantly consulted about the development of the service. Florence's interest in military nursing was not, at one time, confined to England. During the Franco-Prussian War of 1870 she had the curious experience, so great was her reputation, of receiving appeals for her advice from both sides of the front. The French authorities applied to her for plans of a temporary field hospital, while the Crown Princess of Prussia, Queen Victoria's eldest daughter, who was always Florence's ardent disciple, also requested her help. The Princess even asked Florence to supply her with an English nurse to establish a Prussian war hospital on English lines and she had chosen one of her ablest pupils, Miss F. Lees, the same who was later to be distinguished as a District Nurse, to undertake this work. The Princess and Florence were in constant correspondence during this war and Florence gave her many practical hints about the actual running of a hospital in action. It was during this same year, 1870, that the National Society for Aid to the Sick and Wounded, later called the British Red Cross Society, was founded. At the inaugural meeting a letter from Florence was read in which she gave great encouragement to the founders, but stressed the difficulties of work in military hospitals, saying that those who volunteered to serve in them must be 'not sentimental enthusiasts but downright lovers of hard work'. Sometimes it is said that Florence 'founded' the Red Cross, but this is not correct; what is true is that the Swiss, Henri Dunant, the real founder, always maintained that the wonderful example of what Florence had done in the Crimea had inspired him to start the whole Red Cross movement. When peace was declared, Florence had perhaps the unique distinction of receiving decorations from *both* belligerents, for the French Société de Secours aux Blessés Militaires conferred its Bronze Cross on her, while from the German Emperor she obtained the Prussian Cross of Merit.

Within the first ten or fifteen years after its foundation, the Nightingale School received requests from hospitals all over the world for trained nurses to start new schools. This was exactly in accordance with Florence's plan, for from the outset she impressed on her pupils that they were 'trained to train'; they were to go forth in their turn as pioneers and superintendents and they were definitely discouraged from doing private nursing. So each request was, as far as possible, answered in the same way. Florence and Mrs. Wardroper would, as in the case of Liverpool, select some outstanding nurse like Agnes Jones and send her, sometimes with a few other nurses, to start the new school. By about 1880 Florence had the satisfaction of seeing 'Nightingales' as matrons in a large proportion of the most important hospitals in the British Isles, while some had been sent to Canada, the United States, Sweden and Germany, to mention but a few out of many countries. As early as 1867 a request was received from a particularly distant part of the Empire which showed how far the fame of St. Thomas's had already spread. Miss Lucy Osburn and five nurses, who were specially picked by Florence, undertook what was then the tremendous voyage to Australia to start a school in the Infirmary at Sydney. From there some of the original band went in their turn to found other training schools in different parts of Australia.

As each nurse passed out from the parent school to take up her new post, Florence kept in the closest possible touch with her. She constantly wrote letters of encouragement or advice (or even admonition if she thought it was needed!) to her 'daughters' who were scattered so far and wide, and she took the keenest interest in all they told her of their work. In Florence each nurse knew that she had an unchanging and true friend who, however busy she might be, could always find time for a letter and was ready to give help in every difficulty whether it were important or trivial. One nurse told a friend that she had had over two hundred letters from the Lady-in-Chief. For those nurses who were working in London she was always accessible and, besides encouraging them to pay her visits, she frequently had them to stay with her for rest or convalescence. After 1872, when the Nightingale School had moved to the new St. Thomas's and had grown considerably in numbers, her visitors from it became even more numerous. A visit to Florence was considered a great privilege and one of her nurses has charmingly described how she went to South Street.

'The visitor was taken up to Miss Nightingale's room; a light, airy curtain-less room—the general effect one of whiteness, simplicity, flowers. The windows opened on to a balcony, where sometimes the sparrows were pecking at a feast of fine breadcrumbs. On her couch—the satin quilt of military scarlet gave a touch of vivid colour —the "Chief" in her soft black gown leant back against her cushions. She wore a white lace shawl over her smoothly parted hair and more than one shawl—of white

lace or finest Shetland wool—over her ample shoulders.
A pencil and note-book usually lay by her hand; and at
her side was a table holding her writing materials—
pamphlets, a Blue Book—and the tall glass of barley
water, set there by the maid, who brought in the table
and tea-tray. . . . I have many memories of those visits to
Miss Nightingale. She spoke of many things. She very
seldom spoke to me of incidents or persons connected
with the Crimean War; but then it was with intense feeling—almost in a whisper. More often she was interested
in what was going on at the moment. . . . Always the
"statistician", she put questions to her visitor: and it was
rather disturbing to see the pencil and note-book come
into use and one's answers carefully written down.'

This habit of note-taking when she saw her nurses was
forced upon Florence by circumstances (but it also suited
her habit of mind) in order to retain this close personal
touch with every member of the school. She was not
living among her pupils and could not be expected to
remember everything about everybody, so she had to
keep some record of each nurse's visit. To this record she
could afterwards refer, as it helped her and Mrs. Wardroper to choose the right person when some post had to
be filled. As soon as her caller had left her, Florence jotted
down in pencil what she felt to be the most important
points to remember. A great number of these pencilled
memoranda have survived; they consist of a few terse
observations about the nurse herself and then some notes
as to what training experience she had had and in which
wards. In this way Florence could also keep an eye on the
teaching and the practical experience the pupils were receiving, and judge whether the school was being kept up

to her exacting standard. A few examples will suffice to show what these notes were like:

'Nurse T. A most capable little woman. No education, but one can't find it in one's heart to regret it. She seems as good as she can be, but regrets want of education. Not conceited; no complaints. An enthusiasm for her work and for the Sisters. Likes the bustle and hard work of a Surgical Ward.

'Nurse U. Not intelligently active enough for a Sister. No love for her work. If there is anything in her it requires a hand pump to get it out. Appears to know nothing about Ward-Management. Nor about bandaging. Nor about note-taking.

'Nurse V. As self-comfortable but kindly a jack-ass (or Joan-ass) as ever I saw. Thinks she does everything well. Gets up early to misinform herself. Has "done her Notes very well" (her notes scanty, illegible, ill spelt, no grammar). Flighty. Flirty; not thorough. No use.

'Nurse W. Most spiritual and interesting. A green young saint. . . .

'Nurses X, Y, Z. These young ladies rush about the patients not as intelligent women but as maids; they have neither the strong personal benevolent interest in the individual nor the active intellectual interest in the case, nor the pleasure in good ward management that we used to have. Neither X nor Y tidy in hair.'

By 1892, when she was already seventy-two, one might have thought that even Florence's active mind could have nothing further to contribute to nursing questions. Yet in this very year she successfully started what she called 'Health Missioners', nurses who were, as she planned the scheme, to go into the home and, as well as nursing, teach principles of hygiene. They may truly be considered the forerunners of the Health Visitor of to-day. By starting this scheme Florence gave one more proof of the fact that she rated prevention higher than cure, an attitude which placed her far in advance of most of her contemporaries. Four years later she still had the idea fresh in her mind, for she wrote an article outlining a somewhat similar system for the villages of India which she called Health Missioners for Rural India. Almost the last new association for extending the field of nursing to which Florence gave active support was the Victorian Order of Nurses which was started in Canada in 1897 to commemorate Queen Victoria's Diamond Jubilee. Florence embraced the idea with the zest of an old campaigner and in 1898 wrote a letter on the subject to the Marchioness of Aberdeen whose husband was then the Governor-General of Canada. This letter was printed as a booklet and widely circulated.

Towards the end of her life a movement arose in the nursing profession of which Florence thoroughly disapproved. In 1887 the younger generation of nurses thought that the time had come when their already very considerable numbers justified an attempt to foster by organization a feeling of responsibility to the profession. They also felt that some sort of recognition of their training by the government was necessary to improve their status and so they worked hard to obtain State Registration. The whole idea of registration was contrary to Florence's ideas. She maintained to her dying day that nursing was an art and a *vocation*, and she nowhere expressed her views better than in the oft-quoted definition:

'Nursing is an Art; and if it is to be made an art, requires as exclusive a devotion, as hard a preparation, as any painter's or sculptor's work; for what is the having to do with dead canvas or cold marble compared with having to do with the living body—the temple of God's spirit. It is one of the Arts; I had almost said, the finest of the Fine Arts.'

As this was Florence's view of what nursing really meant, it was perhaps natural that she feared that the 'vocational' spirit would no longer be found in each nurse's work. She was convinced that the qualities that go to make the best nurse can never be 'registered' and that any attempt to do so would lead to the nurses being regimented and losing the true spirit of their calling. So she fought the movement with all the weight of her still considerable prestige. It would be out of place here to give details of the registration controversy, but it is important to realize how Florence felt about what has now become a common-place in most countries, in order fully to understand her character.

At the beginning of the present century Florence's work as a nursing *pioneer* was at an end. The fifty-odd years during which she had done everything in her power to promote the training of nurses and the expansion of nursing were over and the Foundress could look back with pride on her work. Since her death nursing has gone into new fields, such as industry, where it was not found in her day, but every extension of the work of nurses, provided they held fast to her ideals, would have met with her approval.

CHAPTER SEVEN

Florence Nightingale's Work for India

After the Nightingale School had been successfully launched and was not claiming all her time, Florence started on an entirely new piece of work. This work was connected with India, and when she began it she possessed no more information regarding the administration and the problems of that country than any other well-educated Englishwoman. Yet she ended by having an intimate knowledge of all Indian matters and the task which began by being of very limited scope expanded so continually and became so intricate and absorbing that in the end she devoted many years of her life to it.

To-day this part of Florence's life's work is all but unknown and is overshadowed by her brilliant achievement in the Crimea and what she did for nursing. Yet her labour for India extended over a long period and was, in her own estimation, the most important and constructive that she ever accomplished. Furthermore, she was considered in her lifetime a great authority on all Indian questions. It is difficult at the present time to appreciate fully the importance of what Florence did for India. The main reason of this difficulty is that, since India and Pakistan are now independent countries, it is only older people who can remember what an important part India once formed of the British Empire, or what a large proportion of the whole

British Army was always on Indian soil. Yet it is interesting to study Florence's connection with India, since this part of her activities shows almost better than any other, the force of her character and the extent of her knowledge as well as her methods of working. Where her Indian work is concerned Florence furnishes an almost unique example of how someone, if endowed with a brilliant brain and colossal powers of application, can make herself an expert on a country without ever visiting it.

Florence's work for India was a direct consequence of what she had done after the Crimean War for the health of the British Army. Her very first contact with Indian affairs was in the earlier part of 1859. Conditions in the British Army in India had been found to be unsatisfactory, so it was suggested that a new Royal Commission be appointed to investigate the matter. The authorities concerned did not wish to have another popular outcry about the neglect of the soldiers such as had arisen after the Crimean War. Every official involved knew what unique first-hand knowledge Florence possessed on everything to do with military hygiene and sanitation, so she was, almost automatically, asked to give her help. Once again she was not an actual member of this Royal Commission, since popular prejudice against women members had not yet been overcome, and once again she did most of the work.

The task which this new Commission had been appointed to carry out was after Florence's own heart. It appealed first of all to her feelings, for she took a deep personal interest in the health and welfare of every individual soldier wherever he might be serving. It also appealed to her intellect, for she knew that it would be a tremendous undertaking and would demand all her powers of observation and her grasp of detail. Even Florence did not perhaps quite realize just how extensive the task was to become, or foresee that what began as work merely for the Army in India would end by being work for the whole country.

To Florence it was a great day when, in May 1859, Queen Victoria signed the Warrant which appointed what was officially called the Royal Commission on the Sanitary State of the Army in India. The Chairman was Sidney Herbert and Florence's former colleagues, Dr. Sutherland and Dr. Farr, were also members. When the Warrant had been signed Florence could openly begin her work, although she had already set on foot some inquiries. The method she used in making these inquiries was very much like that of any trained investigator of the present day, but was much in advance of her time. She saw that the Commissioners, before they could do anything constructive, must know the true facts about what conditions really were like at that moment in India. So Florence drew up a detailed list of questions on various points—a 'Questionnaire' as we should now call it—and arranged that it should be sent to all Stations in India where troops were quartered. In every case the answers to the questionnaire had to be signed by the commanding officer, the engineer officer and the medical officer. This was the situation in about 1860 and then sufficient time had to be allowed to pass before all the replies could be received from India. It was necessarily a slow business as there was then no air mail. As each questionnaire was returned, the answers it contained had to be tabulated, compared, annotated and finally put into a form from which recommendations could afterwards be made. It is to be feared that the persons to whom these questionnaires had been sent did not always return such detailed answers to the various questions as the exacting Florence could have wished. Nevertheless, from what information they received, she and her colleagues compiled a vast amount of material from which they could then draw conclusions and, later, make constructive suggestions. So the work, which must often have been very tedious, went slowly on and during the whole time Florence was its inspiration and presiding genius.

Almost four years elapsed between the date on which the questionnaires had been sent out and that on which the Report was actually published. Throughout all these years Florence and her colleagues had daily devoted hours of labour to the subject. It was characteristic of Florence that she was soon determined to go further than the original 'terms of reference' of the Commission which were, strictly speaking, only concerned with the health of the Army in India. With her usual wide vision Florence had clearly seen that any improvements that could be effected in the health of the troops would be valueless unless they were matched by similar efforts to improve the sanitary condition of the vast civilian population of India. In a word, Florence felt that everyone in India ought to benefit equally from these improved sanitary conditions. To achieve this she knew that the government departments concerned must be induced to co-operate. She fully realized that there might be rocks ahead (and there were!) before the War Office, the India Office and the Government of India would agree to join in this vast work of sanitary reform. Florence was quite undaunted;

she said: 'Done in some way or other, I am determined it shall be,' and in the end it was done, after many difficulties had been overcome.

When this Indian Report finally appeared in print the Commissioners and Florence could at last see the fruit of their arduous labour. Although every official knew that Florence had done the greater part of the writing, there is no portion that actually bears her signature except a section with the clumsy title: 'Observations by Miss Nightingale on the Evidence contained in the Stational Returns.' The subsequent history of this Report is a very good illustration of how Florence was frustrated and hampered in accomplishing this important piece of work. It also shows how, by great determination and not a little diplomacy, she overcame, using methods peculiar to herself, difficulties which would have seemed insuperable to anyone else.

The Report, which ended by being two formidable folio volumes each containing over a thousand pages, was, of course, available to the Press and to Members of Parliament. Yet Florence was quite shrewd enough to realize that very few people would have the time, or take the trouble, to wade through such a mass of material. So she welcomed the fact that the gist of the Report was to be officially reprinted in an abridged form. Imagine her consternation when she found that her 'Observations', which contained the most unsparing criticism of Indian administration, had been omitted in this reprint, whether to shield the incompetent or not she had no means of knowing. But Florence was not the woman to be daunted by what many would have regarded as a tremendous setback. She quickly had the 'Observations' printed at her own expense as a separate book, and circulated this book as widely as she could, both in England and in India. She then saw that this was not enough and that she must go a step farther. So she next persuaded the officials concerned to allow her to make a *revised* abridgement of the original Report. No one supervised Florence's work, so this time she was careful to include her 'Observations' and she also wrote a fresh 'Abstract of the Evidence', because she considered that this had been inaccurately done in the first abridgement. She finally followed all this up by organizing an intensive Press campaign in support of her new abridged Report which would have done credit to any politician of any period.

The *Observations* caused quite a stir among all classes of readers; in fact, after *Notes on Nursing* it was the most popular and widely read of all Florence's books. She next thought of other ways in which she could stimulate interest in Indian questions among an even wider public. In October 1863 she contributed a paper to a Social Science meeting which had the arresting title: 'How men may live and not die in India.' The paper aroused great interest and much discussion and at the end of the session at which it was read (not of course by her) there were 'Three cheers for Miss Nightingale'. Everyone began to realize that on all Indian questions Florence was a power with which, in the future, every administrator must reckon.

After trying to ensure that every official, both at home and in India, had a copy of her abridged Report, Florence was ready to meet the next difficulty which was indeed formidable. From long observation of government methods she feared that the Report would merely be shelved, and that all the years of work which she and her colleagues had devoted to it would accomplish nothing. So she wished to ensure that the recommendations in the Report would be carried out, for she realized that they would otherwise be valueless. Her practical mind quickly grasped the fact that conditions in India would remain as they were unless all civilian administrators, as well as all Army officials, would unite in a great effort to improve them. Her ideal was to see everyone throughout the whole large continent of India living under the best possible hygienic conditions.

This extension of the sphere of her Indian work brought Florence many new friends and correspondents. Among the first of these was Sir John Lawrence (afterwards Lord Lawrence) who was appointed Viceroy in December 1863. He paid Florence a long visit before leaving for India and they discussed together the best means of improving Indian sanitation. She remained in particularly close touch with him, and during all his Viceroyalty they corresponded frequently on everything to do with Indian affairs. After this other viceroys came to see her before they took up their appointment and also wrote to her from India; in fact, her friend, Dr. Jowett, jokingly called her 'Governess of the Governor of India'. Florence soon had many friends among every class of official in India, and they frequently wrote to her for advice on a variety of topics. Later she got in touch with various distinguished Indians, and not only corresponded with them on all matters affecting Indian sanitation, but also received visits from them when they came to London. In the end Florence's knowledge of India became so encyclopaedic that no one there could believe that she had acquired it all by persistent study in London, and at one time a legend was current that she had actually paid the country a visit.

From 1863, when the Indian Report was published, until about 1893, or for a period of some thirty years, Florence watched from her room in South Street the gradual development of Indian sanitation. She laboured incessantly for the improvement of the conditions under which the troops worked in India; indeed she could have earned the title of 'Providence of the Indian Army'. She might with almost equal truth have been called the 'Providence of the Indian peasant', for she so persistently preached two things: first the gospel of irrigation to improve the land and thereby the general well-being of the country folk, and secondly that of pure water, adequate drainage and other sanitary measures to ensure the hygiene of the towns. Her reputation in India as well as in England was very great and she was continually consulted by Indian as well as by British officials. In 1870 she wrote to an Indian correspondent:

'For eleven years past, what little I could do for India, for the conditions on which the Eternal has made to depend the lives and health and social happiness of men, as well Native as European, has been the constant object of my thoughts.'

She was not exaggerating when she wrote these words, for India had always a great claim on her affections and her work had touched every corner of Indian life.

CHAPTER EIGHT

Her Other Interests and Some of Her Friends

By her own inclination as much as from force of circumstance the greater part of Florence Nightingale's life was passed in work connected with nursing and hospitals, and it is as a nurse and a sanitarian that she is chiefly remembered. Of the two, nursing was always her main interest and the object nearest to her heart, yet she was considered almost as much of an authority on sanitation, on the construction of hospitals and on the hygiene of the Army, as on purely nursing questions. Her work for India alone would have gained her fame had she accomplished nothing else. It would, however, be wrong to assume that these were the only subjects which she considered important. In actual fact she was deeply interested in many other topics, and her versatility was so great that she might, had she wished, have become famous in other fields. What makes Florence's career difficult fully to understand is that for almost fifty years she had such diverse interests and worked at so many subjects *simultaneously* that it is often difficult to separate them. In one and the same year she might devote a great deal of time to several unconnected matters and only she herself knew how much she had spent on each.

One of Florence's greatest interests was in statistics, especially after her return from the Crimea. She was naturally of an accurate turn of mind and in the hospitals at Scutari she had noted with horror the confusion that could ensue where the records about patients, including details about their diseases, were either not kept at all or else kept inaccurately. She pleaded with special urgency that the hospitals should use a better system of statistics, and herself drew up a Model Hospital Statistical Form, which she hoped might be universally adopted. She had been made, in 1858, a member of the Statistical Society of England, and when an International Statistical Congress met in London in 1860 she contributed a paper on 'Hospital Statistics' and wrote another for the Social Science Congress in Dublin the next year. In her book, *Notes on Hospitals*, she devoted considerable space to the subject. True to her desire to see correct statistics used everywhere, she worked hard to induce the Home Secretary to require fuller information on the Census papers. Although nothing was done when she first brought the subject up at the 1861 Census, most of her suggestions were afterwards adopted. In later life she hoped to found a Chair of Applied Statistics at Oxford so that the subject should receive the attention which she felt it merited. Her friend, Dr. Jowett, the famous Master of Balliol College, Oxford, was as keenly interested in the subject as she was, but unlike most of Florence's schemes it was never carried out.

Florence was never what is called a 'party politician', but her own experience and convictions made her in favour of Women's Suffrage. She never, however, took any active part in the movement, or worked for it, as she did for so many other causes. Very early in her career she made this private note: 'I must strive after a better life for woman,' and in as far as the possession of a vote might help in the attainment of this 'better life', she was in favour of it. To John Stuart Mill, himself an advocate of the enfranchisement of women, she wrote in 1867: 'That women should have the suffrage, I think no one can be more deeply convinced than I. It is so important for a woman to be a "person" as you say. . . . But it will be years before you obtain the suffrage for women. And in the meantime there are evils which press much more hardly on women than the want of the suffrage.' Furthermore, true to the emphasis she consistently laid on service, it was the responsibilities rather than the privileges attached to having a vote that she stressed. Her point of view on the question of 'women's rights' is well illustrated by a letter written to Madame Mohl shortly after the Crimean War, in which she says: 'I am brutally indifferent to the wrongs or the rights of my sex. And I should have been equally so to any controversy as to whether women ought, or ought not, to do what I have done for the Army; though a woman, having the opportunity and *not* doing it, ought, I think, to be burnt alive.'

Since her deep religious faith was the mainspring of Florence's character, it is natural that she had a lifelong and profound interest in all questions of religion and philosophy. This interest she probably owed to her father, for from the time that she was quite a girl he had always enjoyed discussing such questions with her. All through her long life she seems to have found such questions absorbing and to have derived much spiritual strength from her extensive reading on religious topics. This reading was not only an inspiration but afforded her welcome mental relaxation from the dry and factual tasks on which she was continually engaged. With various friends she corresponded at great length on all these matters. While Aunt Hannah had been the principal recipient of such letters when Florence was a girl, in later life she discussed these topics in very great detail with her Aunt Mai and with her close friend, Dr. Jowett. Many letters to both of them are entirely devoted to such discussions.

To give details about every subject in which Florence was interested would be quite beyond the scope of this book, but one last interest may be recorded since it affords a perfect example of how her trained and lucid mind could tackle some unfamiliar subject, master it and then make constructive suggestions regarding it. Her attention had been drawn to the plight of the aborigines, who are the primitive races in Australia, Africa and various parts of the Empire. A question had arisen as to whether the decline and imminent extinction of these races was due to the system under which they were being educated by the British. This was quite enough to start Florence off on a new line of research. She collected a great mass of data on the subject, obtained (of course) all the available statistics regarding the native schools, sifted the information with her wonted thoroughness, and incorporated it in a paper called, characteristically, 'Sanitary Statistics of Colonial Schools', which was read at a Social Science meeting. This paper was one more variation on her usual theme—that sanitary defects were the root of the trouble—and it aroused a great deal of discussion. She never appears to have gone any further with this particular subject, but may justly claim to have been one of the people who helped to arrest, if she did not prevent, the threatened extinction of these peoples.

If Florence showed variety in her activities she showed it scarcely less in her choice of friends. They were as diverse in their interests as they were in their professions and social standing—in fact, their only common denominator was often their devotion to Florence. For she was one of those women who have the genius for friendship and of inspiring in many a lifelong devotion, while by some she was almost idolized. Her friends may be roughly divided into two groups, those who knew her well in the days before she had become a national figure, and those who, as well as being her friends, were for many years her colleagues and co-workers. To the former class belonged, besides her adored relations, Aunt Mai, Marianne Nicholson and Hilary Bonham Carter, such intimates as Madame Mohl and particularly Mrs. Bracebridge; to the latter notably Dr. Sutherland. Such men as Sir John McNeill, Colonel Tulloch, Sir Douglas Galton and Mr. Rathbone were also closely allied to Florence through associating with her in some piece of government or nursing work. Florence was deeply attached to her brother-in-law, Sir Harry Verney, and over a long period he gave her devoted assistance, not only with her official work but especially with the Nightingale School. For many years he was Chairman of the Council of the Nightingale Fund and was keenly interested in the progress of the Nightingale School. It owed scarcely less to another of Florence's close relatives, her first-cousin, Mr. Henry Bonham Carter. He served as Secretary of the Nightingale Fund for over forty years and during all those years was always ready with his advice and help at every stage of the school's development. Throughout her career Florence possessed an almost unique power of making her relations as enthusiastic as herself about her interests.

Two of Florence's circle stood rather in a class by themselves, Sidney Herbert and Benjamin Jowett. Sidney Herbert and his wife had known Florence for many years before she went to the Crimea and his long collaboration with her during the Royal Commissions is an association unique in the annals of friendship. Dr. Jowett, on the other hand, occupied quite a different place in her life. They were never co-workers, but he watched every phase of her work with lively interest for about thirty years and it was to him that she could turn for sympathy in its ups and downs. It was to him, rather than to any other friend, that she felt able fully to open her mind on religion and discuss questions of metaphysics and philosophy. He was also the only person whose advice she never resented and sometimes even followed.

It was not only her old friends who rejoiced in the privilege of knowing Florence. She seems to have had the power of charming new acquaintances who fell under her spell even at their first meeting. 'She is a noble-minded woman and so charming,' said one of them, while another expressed much the same feeling by saying: 'She is so far more delightful in herself than in one's imagination.' One of the secrets of this charm may have been that she was a good listener and that, although so vehement with the pen, in conversation she was thoughtful and earnest but very restrained and never found it necessary to raise the voice that all who remember her describe as gentle and well-modulated. But perhaps the strongest reason why everyone loved Florence was because of her unfailing loyalty. Her friends knew that she would never forget them and that her affection would remain unchanged. To someone like Florence to whom her friends meant so much it was a misfortune that by the very fact of her longevity she outlived them all. Yet in each generation of nurses she could in a certain measure renew her youth and, although they could never take the place of old friends, they kept her interest in life fresh and vivid.

CHAPTER NINE

Florence Nightingale's Writings

No biography of Florence Nightingale would be complete without a brief account of her writings, since one can truly say that during the greater part of her long life the pen was seldom out of her hand. The sheer amount of what she wrote is quite stupendous and would probably astonish anyone who has never seen a list of her writings. Yet unfortunately her literary work is peculiarly tantalizing, since the greater part is in official publications which are not readily accessible to the ordinary reader.

It is not easy to know what Florence herself felt about being an author. When she was a young woman she seems to have set little store by it, for at twenty-four she wrote to her dear friend, Mary Clarke: 'You ask me why I do not write something. I think what is not of the first class had better not exist at all, and besides, I had so much rather live than write—writing is only a substitute for living. . . . I think one's feelings waste themselves in words, they ought all to be distilled into actions, and into actions which bring results.' But, somewhat later, she seems to have realized that, had she chosen, she could have made writing her profession, for we find this entry in a diary of 1850: 'I had three paths among which to choose; I might have been a literary woman, or a married woman,

121

or a Hospital Sister.' In her private memoranda there are allusions to 'Works', among which there may have been a novel, although no trace of it was found among her papers. In the end Florence turned away from the possibilities of a literary career, perhaps because she felt that her family wished to 'side-track' her into writing as being so much more 'respectable' than the nursing on which she had set her heart. Later in life one of her friends at any rate took her writing seriously. Benjamin Jowett suggested to her that she should put her collected notes on religious topics into a suitable shape for publication and also urged her to complete some work she had already begun on the writings of some of the medieval mystics. This she seems at one moment to have felt inclined to

3. Florence Nightingale's Handwriting, 1879

undertake, but shortly afterwards her father's death, in 1874, coupled with pressure of other work made her put it aside and she never afterwards attempted it. True to her youthful dictum that writing should be 'distilled into actions', most of her written work was in official publications; indeed every piece of government work that she carried out involved writing in some shape or form. In other words, her writing was always conditioned by her work or, more briefly, her writing was her work. It must also never be forgotten that, when we speak of writing being Florence's 'work', it was work in a very real sense. Anyone undertaking such an immense amount of literary composition in these days would have one or even several efficient secretaries to help her and not be forced to do overmuch actual writing herself. But Florence possessed no such mitigation of her labours. She had constant assistance from various devoted friends such as Aunt Mai, A. H. Clough and Dr. Sutherland, and experts were always ready to place their valuable knowledge at her disposal. But the bulk of the actual writing in her vast literary activity was done by her own hand, a fact that was revealed to those who may not previously have realized it by the mass of manuscript material found after her death. Her handwriting is uniformly excellent, not to say beautiful, although it varies a little according as to whether Florence is using pen or pencil, the whole form of her script in pencil being more upright. To show you how well she wrote, a specimen of her handwriting in 1879 is reproduced on page 122.

With so much official writing to do, it would be interesting to know how much Florence enjoyed composing a book for its own sake. We can safely assume that she did derive pleasure from producing *Notes on Nursing* and *Notes on Hospitals* and the religious book already alluded to, with the long title of *Suggestions for Thought to the Searchers after Truth among the Artizans of England*. It is an interesting indication of where her main interest lay that the very first thing from her pen to appear in print was the tiny booklet called *The Institution of Kaiserswerth on the Rhine*, which gave a short account of the Fliedners' work and the training of the Deaconesses.

Her large share in the Report of 1858 has already been mentioned, but none of her contemporaries, unless they were her very close friends, or in official circles, realized just how large this share had been. Her long private report also reached only a limited circle of readers. Although it is little known, this book—*Notes on Matters affecting the Health, Efficiency and Hospital Administration of the British Army*—is the most monumental piece of writing Florence ever undertook and has been justly called the 'most remarkable but least known of her works'. The chief reason why it has never been well known, either in 1858 or since, is that, like many of Florence's other writings, it was never 'published' in the sense that we talk about publishing a book. It was privately printed at her own expense to 'circulate among influential people'. When one considers that this enormously lengthy book, which contains over eight hundred pages, was written in six months (February to August, 1857) when Florence was in very poor health and had only some assistance from Aunt Mai and A. H. Clough, it is difficult which to admire more, her amazing intellectual grasp or her capacity for intensive work.

Whatever her intimates may have felt, the general public could form no opinion of Florence's powers as a writer until, in 1859, she had published *Notes on Nursing*. With this she leapt at once into literary fame. *Notes on Nursing* was then, and still is, the best-known book that Florence ever wrote, and many have read it who know little about its author. When it appeared most people thought that she had retired into private life and this book brought about a renewal of her popularity. It was from the outset a 'best-seller', as 15,000 copies were bought in the first month. No book of exactly that kind had ever been written before, and it remains even to-day the best description of what one might call the fundamental principles of nursing. But perhaps in 1859 some people found the *Notes* a little disturbing. It must have given an equal shock on the one hand to those who took a 'sentimental' view of nurses, and on the other to those who regarded nursing as an occupation fit only for servants, about which no book need be written. The very chapter headings must have puzzled her readers and were a challenge to contemporary views about the sick-room. Into the Victorian stuffiness blew the fresh air of Florence's modern ideas about ventilation. What they could think about an authoress who chose to divide her book into such sections as: 'Ventilation and Warming', 'Health of Houses', or 'Cleanliness of Rooms and Walls', when they had (perhaps) expected some pretty conceit about the beauty of attendance at the sick-bed! But still, the book was by that famous nurse, Florence Nightingale, and so they read on, and as they saw how true were the authoress's remarks, bewilderment turned to admiration. From every quarter came praise of the *Notes*; Queen Victoria 'thanked Miss Nightingale *very much* for the book', while the Grand

Duchess of Baden, daughter of Emperor William I, wrote: 'I will not attempt to describe to you with how much interest and admiration I read these pages.' Perhaps the tribute Florence valued most was that of the distinguished doctor, Sir James Paget, who said: 'I am ashamed to find how much I have learnt from the *Notes*, more, I think, than from any other book of the same size that I have ever read.' It seems likely that although *Notes on Nursing* was written all at one time it was a compilation of notes and observations that Florence had been making for many years, notably during her time in the East. She may never have had time even to jot down these observations, but her naturally good memory helped her to recall examples within her own experience to illustrate the points she wished to make. One feels while reading it that the book is written by a practical nurse and not merely by a clever woman theorizing at her writing table.

Notes on Nursing is written in a lively, almost racy style and combines general principles with minute attention to detail in a way that is the true hall-mark of all Florence's work. It is enlivened too with many touches of caustic humour. What must Victorian young ladies have thought about the way Florence laughed at a current definition of a nurse?

'No *man*, not even a doctor, gives any other definition of what a nurse should be than this—"devoted and obedient". This definition would do just as well for a porter. It might even do for a horse. It would not do for a policeman.'

How shocked, too, they must have been at the passage where she condemned some ideas then prevalent on nursing in the words:

'It seems a commonly received idea among men, and even among women themselves, that it requires nothing but a disappointment in love, or incapacity in other things, to turn a woman into a good nurse. This reminds one of the parish where a stupid old man was set to be schoolmaster because "he was past keeping the pigs".'

It is particularly noticeable that Florence never ceased to condemn the wrong motives for wishing to become a nurse and wrote in another connection:

'A woman who takes the sentimental view of nursing (which she calls "ministering", as if she were an angel) is of course worse than useless; a woman possessed with the idea that she is making a sacrifice will never do; and a woman who thinks any kind of nursing work "beneath a nurse" will simply be in the way.'

As this was the attitude towards nursing adopted by a great number of people, Florence must further have jolted many aspirants by her statement:

'It has been said and written scores of times, that every woman makes a good nurse. I believe, on the contrary, that the very elements of nursing are all but unknown.'

She then defined the wider meaning she gave to the term:

'I use the word nursing for want of a better. It has been limited to signify little more than the administration of medicines and the application of poultices. It ought to signify the proper use of fresh air, light, warmth, cleanliness, quiet, and the proper selection and administration of diet—all at the least expense of vital power to the patient.'

However, in spite of what some might think were subversive views, especially that uncomfortable insistence on fresh air, the popularity of the *Notes* continued and it was constantly reprinted. Even to-day one can sometimes pick up copies of early editions of this very modest volume and read it with undiminished interest. It contains about seventy pages and is soberly bound in black cloth.

The next year, 1860, Florence may have felt that she could improve the book, for a second revised edition was published. A little later it was translated into French, German and Italian. *Notes on Nursing* was rather expensive as it originally cost five shillings, which would be more like fifteen shillings by present-day values, and perhaps its authoress felt that it could be useful to people who could not afford this sum. So in 1861 she brought out *Notes on Nursing for the Labouring Classes*, a tiny paper-bound book which only cost sevenpence. It was adapted from the original *Notes* and was so small it could easily be carried about. Florence may have felt that some younger people might read her book in this newer form, so she added a chapter specially for girls called 'Minding Baby'. The style is simple and friendly, and it is one of the earliest as well as one of the best things ever written about the handling of little children. Florence had seen many little girls near her home trying to be good 'little mothers' to their baby brothers and sisters, just as she had been long ago to her beloved little cousin, Shore, and she wanted to tell them some things she thought might help them in language that they could understand. This delightful chapter is added at the end of the present book so that we can all read and enjoy it.

The other book that Florence published in 1859, *Notes on Hospitals*, also dealt with matters that had hitherto received but scant attention. In her challenging way Florence began the book with the startling sentence: 'It may seem a strange principle to enunciate as the very first requirement in a hospital that it should do the sick no harm.' No one before Florence Nightingale had taken the trouble to state in print how a hospital should be built and why, and both architects and all those connected in any way with hospitals must have felt that here was a new writer who had made a very valuable contribution to an almost unheeded subject.

The Report on the Army in India, which was published in 1863, had involved her in years of ceaseless work, in much detailed writing and in many hours spent in proof-reading and revision. The 'Observations by Miss Nightingale', which forms one part of this Report, is one of her most characteristic pieces of writing; the style is utterly her own, lucid and arresting with not a few touches of trenchant humour. In one passage for example she says of one barracks that: 'We find it stated "The men, three hundred per room, are generally accommodated without inconvenient over-crowding". What is *convenient* over-crowding?' and in another, when discussing the inadequate washing facilities, she remarks: 'If the facilities for washing were as great as those for drink, our Indian army would be the cleanest body of men in the world.' Probably the book, which was widely circulated both in England and in India, did ultimately more good for the men serving in India than any other that was then written. To make the material more likely to be read as well as to prove her points, Florence inserted a few illustrations, for which she paid herself, from sketches sent her from India. Some conventional people may have thought it very frivolous to have pictures in a Blue Book, but on the whole the *Observations* was enthusiastically received and its popularity was only second to *Notes on Nursing*. Florence's writings that deal with India form the largest section numerically of her works. Their range is amazing, although a good number are on subjects that have now lost the topical interest that they had when Florence wrote them. Yet in each one the reader is impressed by her masterly grasp of the subject and by the pains that she took to make even the driest material live.

The next really important piece of writing that Florence undertook, after finishing this Indian Report, was once more government work. This time it was on a subject that was exactly to her taste. She had been deeply concerned at the conditions then prevailing in the Workhouse Infirmaries of London and in 1867 she contributed to the Report on this subject a paper about the nursing. It is one of the best things Florence ever wrote on the subject of training nurses, and she must have felt that it correctly summarized her views as she had it separately printed. A year later Agnes Jones died in harness and Florence wrote an account of her career in a paper called *Good Words*. It is more than an ordinary obituary notice, for it is also an appeal to the young womanhood of England to follow Agnes's noble example. Many girls afterwards told Florence that they had been inspired to become nurses by reading this article.

The next few years were filled for Florence with official writing, mostly on India. To the year 1871 belongs a remarkable book called *Introductory Notes on Lying-in Institutions*, which entailed an immense amount of research. It was not until 1882 that she wrote what are almost the best things on nursing topics that ever came from her pen, namely two articles which she contributed to *Quain's Dictionary of Medicine*. They show not only her interesting scheme of training and the value she set on the highest ideals, but are good examples of her manner of writing. A few years later, when she was already an elderly woman, Florence contributed a paper called 'Sick-Nursing and Health-Nursing' to the Chicago Exhibition of 1893.

One section of Florence's writings falls into a class apart, namely her Addresses to the nurses of the Nightingale and other training schools. Since she was never well enough to come to St. Thomas's and speak to her nurses in person, she occasionally wrote them an Address, or open letter, which was read aloud on some special occasion to the assembled pupils in the school. Copies of the Address, which were sometimes a facsimile of her handwriting, were presented to them afterwards. The first one was prepared in 1872. Florence's style of writing is more discursive in these Addresses than in her other prose and there are, inevitably, many repetitions. They are valuable in that they give us an insight into what she felt about nursing, since they were written with a set purpose, namely to hold ever before the members of the school the high ideals of their profession. At the time of writing they were not published, but some of them were afterwards issued in book form.

One word more must be said about Florence's religious and philosophic writings because, although forming the smallest section of the total of her literary output, they are sufficient to show both her wide reading about these subjects and her profound interest in them. Perhaps, however, to the modern reader they will always remain the most elusive as well as the smallest section. Like many famous women, such as St. Catherine of Siena and St.

Theresa of Avila, who were statesmen and women of action but also mystics, Florence had likewise a mystical side in her nature that showed itself in religious meditation and an intense interest in religious and philosophic speculation. For many years she made notes and observations on these topics, but never published anything. In 1860 she gathered these rather miscellaneous jottings into the book, *Suggestions for Thought*, already mentioned and had a small issue of one hundred and fifty copies privately printed to present to intimate friends. It is difficult to read since it has the defect of never having been revised; the style is discursive and there are so many repetitions that it would be unfair to judge from this book alone what Florence's capacity as a religious writer might have been. Several years later, in 1873, Florence contributed two articles on religious questions to *Fraser's Magazine*, but with them she seems to have exhausted her desire to publish anything on these topics, or possibly she no longer had the time to do them justice.

No account, however brief, of Florence's writings would be complete without mentioning her letters. There must be literally thousands of them in existence of which a very large number are preserved in the British Museum. They are on every conceivable topic and vary in length from a short note to many closely written pages on some special subject. From her girlhood Florence seems to have thought that letters mattered, and to have taken great pains in composing them. In fact, she sometimes felt that her facility in this direction was a snare and she once said: 'That power of always writing a good letter whenever one likes is a great temptation.' When she was pleased with a turn of phrase she might use it in several letters or even in something which was eventually printed. Since she had very few except official visitors, letter-writing was her only means of keeping in touch with her large circle of friends and relations. So while, on some particular day, one letter might be a long and highly technical composition to a government official, another was just as likely to be an affectionate birthday greeting to a young cousin, or a short note of sympathy or advice to one of her nurses.

There is perhaps no better way of gaining an insight into the variety of Florence's interest or of forming a clearer idea both of the force of her intellect and of her tremendous power of mastering a difficult subject than by a study of her literary work, but it would be beyond the scope of this book to mention everything that she ever wrote. The range of the subjects she handled would in itself be remarkable even were the treatment of the material uninspired, but in view of the uniform excellence of her style it is no exaggeration to rank Florence among the outstanding writers of the nineteenth century.

CHAPTER TEN

The Last Years

On 12th May 1900 Florence celebrated her eightieth birthday, and the date was made the occasion for a renewal of the devotion of the old days. Congratulations flowed in from every side and from every kind of person. The large army of trained nurses all over the world also honoured this important anniversary of their leader.

After 1900 the tempo of Florence Nightingale's life slowed down. She was now over eighty and bodily infirmities were beginning to hamper someone who had never been hampered by anything before. In contrast to the years of her middle age her health seems to have improved as she grew older; life's twilight for her was calm and serene and she enjoyed a robust old age. Of her bodily weaknesses the one that troubled her first was the gradual failure of her eyesight. Although she could recognize people and see distant objects, Florence was suddenly faced with an inability to write. She who had sat or lain in her room, pencil in hand, ready to undertake any amount of writing or merely to make notes on any point that interested her during the conversation of some visitor, was now to be seen with those same hands idle.

The disability of not being able to read was also a serious deprivation to someone who had always been an

assiduous reader, but various friends and relations helped
Florence by reading to her, as she now submitted to reading aloud although as a girl she had disliked it. She enjoyed listening to the daily papers and took an interest in
various books, asking the reader to mark any passage
with which she had been particularly struck. While of
necessity she gradually became unable to concentrate on
new topics, there was one interest which she never lost
and that was in the soldiers, 'her children' of the old days.
It is said that even in extreme old age if anyone talked
about them Florence's flagging attention was aroused
when nothing else could interest her.

One or other of Florence's nearest relations often
stayed for long periods at South Street, but in 1902, by
the exercise of some diplomacy, a resident companion
was introduced into the household. She was called 'lady-
housekeeper' but was really a 'private secretary with large
initiative'. It was Miss E. Bosanquet, Florence's secretary
in 1906, who took the cheerful photograph reproduced
on Plate 5. Later, Florence occasionally had the services
of one of her own trained nurses, but it is recorded that
sometimes, after she had been 'tucked up' for the night,
she would fancy herself back at work once more and get
out of bed to 'tuck up' the nurse!

The keynote of Florence's old age was cheerfulness and
serenity, and one of those who saw her frequently in the
last years said that there was an amazing atmosphere of
peace and happiness throughout the house. The years of
struggle and incessant work were now over, and a quiet
contentment had followed them. Florence could still take
an interest in the things around her and got much pleasure,
for example, while she sat in her room, in watching the

birds feeding on the balcony. A few favoured callers were still admitted, especially matrons and nurses, and all of them got this same impression of a contented and happy old lady. Almost one of the last visitors who saw Florence early in 1910 said: 'She was sitting up by the fire in the familiar room, her mind evidently busy with happy thoughts, and once or twice she spoke in a tone of satisfaction.'

Now that Florence's life had passed into its final quiet and peaceful phase, it seemed almost an irony that, where-as no honours or public recognition had been given her in her younger womanhood, they were showered upon her when she was no longer able fully to appreciate them. In December 1907 King Edward VII paid her the great compliment of bestowing upon her the Order of Merit, an Order which he had established a short time before. She was the first woman to receive it and is still the only one to whom it has ever been awarded. As Florence was not strong enough to go to Buckingham Palace and be invested by King Edward in person, the Order was brought to South Street by Sir Douglas Dawson. It is doubtful whether she fully realized what was going on, yet she murmured: 'Too kind, too kind', as though at least understanding that some compliment had been paid her. Earlier in that same year the International Red Cross, at their Congress in London, had sent her a message of congratulation. In the next year the City of London, not to be outdone, conferred the Freedom of the City on Florence in March; the Roll of Freemen was conveyed to her house for her to sign and with great difficulty she appended her initials to it. It seemed paradoxical that, whereas the City could have conferred this distinction on

Florence at any time during the period of some fifty years since her return from the Crimea, it should not have been given until the recipient was fast slipping towards a world where honours have no significance. But even if Florence had fully appreciated the meaning of these various marks of public esteem, she would have preferred to look upon them as a tribute to her work rather than to herself.

The end came very quietly on 13th August 1910 when Florence was slightly over ninety. A burial in Westminster Abbey was suggested, but in accordance with her known wishes the family refused this final honour and instead she lies in her parents' grave in the churchyard of St. Margaret's, East Wellow, in Hampshire, the church which the family had always attended when they were at Embley Park. Her coffin was borne at the funeral by six Guardsmen, a fitting tribute to one who had spent the best years of her life in work for the soldier. On the side of the monument one can read the initials 'F. N.' and the dates, and so in death as in life Florence was true to her principle of shunning publicity.

The full significance of Florence's life and work and her place in history cannot even yet be accurately determined, but with every year that passes her achievements are seen in truer perspective and the stature of her personality becomes the greater. Fame came to her early and this fame survived her death—indeed she remains the most outstanding figure of the whole Crimean campaign. A story is told of how, some years after it was over, a dinner was given to officers who had fought in the Crimean War. Each guest was asked to write on a slip of paper the name of the person whose services during the campaign would be longest remembered by posterity. When the papers were examined each one contained the same name—Florence Nightingale.

There are few monuments to Florence, except for statues in Waterloo Place, London, and at Derby. Her two homes have passed out of the possession of her family, for Lea Hurst is now a holiday home for nurses and Embley Park is a boys' school. Yet we do not need these tangible reminders of Florence's genius. Her true memorial is the profession of nursing, a living monument that has made her name famous all over the globe. But if nursing be her finest memorial it is not her only claim to greatness. What she accomplished in the Crimean War had given her an international reputation, but it occupied a mere two years in a very long life wholly devoted to public service. Had she done nothing else but her work for India or had she accomplished nothing more than her reforms after the Crimean War without initiating modern nursing, she would still have remained enshrined in every English heart. But when such brilliant achievements and so many outstanding qualities are combined in one person, she stands out as one of the greatest women of all time.

List of Events in Florence Nightingale's Life
(Events of general interest are given in italics)

1820   *January, King George IV comes to the Throne.*
        12th May, Florence Nightingale born at Florence, Italy.

1825   Mr. Nightingale buys Embley Park in Hampshire.

1828–30 Florence writes 'La Vie de Florence Rossignol'.

1830   *King William IV comes to the Throne.*

1837   *June, Queen Victoria comes to the Throne.*
        September, Florence goes abroad with her family.

1839   April, the Nightingale family return from abroad.

1845   Florence tries to go to Salisbury Infirmary to train as a nurse.

1847–8 Florence spends the winter in Rome with the Bracebridges.

1849–50 Florence goes to Egypt, Greece, etc., with the Bracebridges.

1850   July, Florence goes for a fortnight to Kaiserswerth.

1851   *The Great Exhibition in Hyde Park, London.*
        July–October, Florence goes again to Kaiserswerth.

1853   Florence starts negotiations to become Superintendent of the Establishment for Gentle-women during illness.

March, Florence works with the Soeurs de Charité in Paris.

August, Florence becomes the Superintendent of the Establishment for Gentlewomen.

1854   *March, War declared on Russia (the Crimean War).*

21st October, Florence starts for Scutari.

5th November, Battle of Inkerman (in the Crimea).

1855   May, Florence visits hospitals in the Crimea and contracts fever.

1856   *March, Peace signed.*

August, Florence returns home.

1856–8   Florence works for the Royal Commission on the Health of the Army.

1858   Report of Commission and Florence's 'Notes', etc, published.

1859   Florence writes 'Notes on Nursing' and 'Notes on Hospitals'.

1860   9th July, Nightingale School, St. Thomas's Hospital, started.

Florence prints her 'Suggestions for Thought'.

1861   2nd August, death of Sidney Herbert.

November, death of Arthur Hugh Clough.

14th December, death of the Prince Consort.

1861–5   *Civil War in the U.S.A.*

1862–3   Florence works for Indian Commission.

1863   Report of Indian Commission published.

1864   *Convention of Geneva signed and start of the International Red Cross.*

1865   May, Agnes Jones goes into Brownlow Hill Infirmary, Liverpool.

1867	Florence works at the reform of Workhouse Infirmary nursing in London.
1870	*Franco-Prussian War.*
1871	Florence writes 'Introductory Notes on Lying-in Institutions'.
1872	Florence writes the first Address to the Nightingale School.
1874	Death of Mr. Nightingale.
1880	Death of Mrs. Nightingale.
1882	Florence writes articles for 'Quain's Dictionary of Medicine'.
1883	Florence awarded the Royal Red Cross.
1893	Death of Benjamin Jowett.
1894	Death of Sir Harry Verney and Mr. William Shore Smith.
	Florence writes an article for the Congress at Chicago.
1896	Embley Park sold.
1900	12th May, Florence receives congratulations on her eightieth birthday.
1901	*January, King Edward VII comes to the Throne.*
1907	June, Florence honoured by the Red Cross Congress in London.
	December, Florence awarded the Order of Merit.
1908	March, Florence given Freedom of the City of London.
1910	*May, King George V comes to the Throne.*
	13th August, Florence dies in her sleep in London.

APPENDIX II

'Minding Baby'
(from *Notes on Nursing* by Florence Nightingale)

And now, girls, I have a word for you. You and I have all had a great deal to do with 'minding baby', though 'baby' was not our own baby. And we would all of us do a great deal for baby, which we would not do for ourselves.

Now, all that I have said about nursing grown-up people applies a great deal more to nursing baby. For instance, baby will suffer from a close room when you don't feel that it is close. If baby sleeps even for a few hours, much more if it is for nights and nights—in foul air, baby will, without any doubt whatever, be puny and sickly, and most likely to have measles or scarlatina, and not get through it well.

Baby will feel want of fresh air more than you. Baby will feel cold much sooner than you. Above all, baby will suffer more from not being kept clean (only see how it enjoys being washed in nice luke-warm water). Baby will want its clothes and its bed-clothes changed oftener than you. Baby will suffer more from a dirty house than you. Baby *must* have a cot to itself; else it runs the risk of being over-laid or suffocated. Baby must not be covered up too much in bed, nor too little. The same when it is up. And you must look after these things. Mother is perhaps too busy to see whether baby is too much muffled up or too little.

You must take care that baby is not startled by loud sudden noises; all the more you must not wake it in this way out of its sleep. Noises which would not frighten you, frighten baby.

And many a sick baby has been killed in this way.

You must be very careful about its food; about being strict to the minute for feeding it; not giving it too much at a time (if baby is sick after its food, you *have* given it too much). Neither must it be under-fed. Above all, never give it any unwholesome food, nor anything at all to make it sleep, unless the doctor orders it.

If you knew how many, even well-to-do, babies I have known who have died from having had something given to make them sleep, and 'keep them quiet'—not the first time, nor the second, nor the tenth time, perhaps—but at last.

I could tell you many true stories, which have all happened within my own knowledge, of mischief to babies from their nurses neglecting these things.

Here are a few:

1. Baby, who is weaned, requires to be fed often, regularly, and not too much at a time.

I know a mother whose baby was in great danger one day from convulsions. It was about a year old. She said she had wished to go to church; and so, before going, had given it its three meals in one. Was it any wonder that the poor little thing had convulsions?

I have known (in Scotland) a little girl, not more than five years old, whose mother had to go great distances every day, and who was trusted to feed and take care of her little brother, under a year old. And she always did it right. She always did what mother told her. A stranger coming into the hut one day (it was no better than a hut) said: 'You will burn baby's mouth.' 'Oh, no,' she said, 'I always burn my own mouth first.'

2. When I say, be careful of baby, I don't mean have it always in your arms. If the baby is old enough, and the weather warm enough for it to have some heat in itself, it is much better for a child to be crawling about than to be always in its little nurse's arms. And it is much better for it to amuse itself than to have her always making noises to it.

The healthiest, happiest, liveliest, most beautiful baby I ever saw was the only child of a busy laundress. She washed all day in a room with the door open upon a larger room, where she put the child. It sat or crawled upon the floor all day, with no other play-fellow than a kitten, which it used to hug. Its mother kept it beautifully clean, and fed it with perfect regularity. The child was never frightened at anything. The room where it sat was the house-place; and it always gave notice to its mother when anybody came in, not by a cry, but by a crow. I lived for many months within hearing of that child, and never heard it cry day or night.

I think there is a great deal too much of amusing children now; and not enough of letting them amuse themselves.

Never distract a child's attention. If it is looking at one thing, don't show it another; and so on.

3. At the same time, dullness and especially want of light, is worse for children than it is for you.

A child was once brought up quite alone in a dark room, by persons who wished to conceal its being alive. It never saw any one, except when it was fed; and though it was treated perfectly kindly, it grew up an idiot. This you will easily guess.

Plenty of light, and sunlight particularly, is necessary to make a child active, and merry, and clever. But, of all things, don't burn baby's brains out by letting the sun bake its head when out, especially in its little cart, on a hot summer's day.

Never leave a child in the dark; and let the room it lives in be *always* as light as possible, and as sunny. Except, of course, when the doctor tells you to darken the room, which he will do in some children's illnesses.

4. Do you know that one-half of all the nurses in service are girls of from five to twenty years old? You see, you are very important little people. Then there are all the girls who are nursing mother's baby at home; and, in all these cases, it seems pretty nearly to come to this, that baby's health for its whole life depends upon you, girls, more than upon anything else.

I need hardly say to you, what a charge! For I believe that you, all of you, or nearly all, care about baby too much not to feel this nearly as much as I do. You, all of you, want to make baby grow up well and happy, if you knew how.

So I say again:

5. The main want of baby is always to have fresh air.

You can make baby ill by keeping the room where it sleeps tight shut up, even for a few hours.

You can kill baby when it *is* ill by keeping it in a hot room, with several people in it, and all the doors and windows shut.

The doctor who looks after the Queen's children says so.

This is the case most particularly when the child has something the matter with its lungs and its breathing.

I found a poor child dying in a small room, tight shut up, with a large fire, and four or five people round it to see it die. Its breathing was short and hurried; and it could not cough up what was choking its lungs and throat—mucus it is called. The doctor, who was a very clever man, came in, set open door and window, turned everybody out but one, and stayed two hours to keep the room clear and fresh. He gave the child no medicine; and it was cured simply by his fresh air.

A few hours will do for baby, both in killing and curing it, what days will not do for a grown-up person.

Another doctor found a child (it was a rich one) dying in a splendid close room, nearly breathless from throat complaint. He walked straight to the window and pulled it open; 'for,' he said, 'when people can breathe very little air, they want that little good.' The mother said he would kill the child. But, on the contrary, the child recovered.

But—

6. Take you care not to let a draught blow upon a child, especially a sick child.

Perhaps you will say to me: 'I don't know what you would have me do. You puzzle me so. You tell me, don't feed the child too much, and don't feed it too little; don't keep the room shut up, and don't let there be a draught; don't let the child be dull, and don't amuse it too much.' Dear little nurse, you must learn to *manage*. Some people never do learn management. I have felt all these difficulties myself; and I can tell you that it is not from reading my book that you will learn to mind baby well, but from practising yourself how best to manage to do what other good nurses (and my book, if you like it) tell you.

But about the draughts.

It is all nonsense what some old nurses say, that you can't give baby fresh air without giving it a chill; and, on the other hand, you may give baby a chill which will kill it (by letting a draught blow upon it when it is being washed, for instance, and chilling its whole body, though only for a moment), without giving it fresh air at all; and depend upon this, the less fresh air you give to its lungs, and the less water you give to its skin, the more liable it will be to colds and chills.

If you can keep baby's air always fresh indoors and out of doors, and never chill baby, you are a good nurse.

A sick baby's skin is often cold, even when the room is quite close. Then you must air the room, and put hot flannels or hot bottles (not too hot) next baby's body; and give it its warm food.

But I have often seen nurses doing just the contrary, namely, shutting up every chink and throwing a great weight of bedclothes over the child, which makes it colder, as it has no heat in itself.

You would just kill a feverish child by doing this.

A children's doctor, very famous in London, says that when a sick child dies, it is just as often an *accident* as not; that is, people kill it by some foolish act of this kind, just as much as if they threw it out of a window. And he says, too, that when a sick child dies suddenly, it is almost always an accident. It might have been prevented. It was *not* that the child was ill, and so its death could not be helped, as people say.

He tells us what brings on these sudden deaths in sick

children: Startling noises; chilling the child's body; wakening it suddenly; feeding it too much or too quickly; altering its posture suddenly, or shaking it roughly; frightening it. And to this you may add (more than anything else, too), *keeping it in foul air, especially when asleep, especially at night*, even for a few hours, and even when you don't feel it yourself. This is, most of all, what kills babies.

Baby's breathing is so tender, so easily put out of order. Sometimes you see a sick baby who seems to be obliged to attend to every breath it draws, and to 'breathe carefully', in order to breathe at all; and if you disturb it rudely, it is all over with baby. Anything which calls upon it for breath may stop it altogether.

7. *Remember to keep baby clean.* I can remember when mothers boasted that *their* 'children's feet had never been touched by water; no, nor any part of them but faces and hands'; that somebody's 'child had had its feet washed, and it never lived to grow up,' etc.

But we know better now. And I daresay you know that to keep every spot of baby's body always clean, and never to let any pore of its tender skin be stopped up by dirt or unwashed perspiration is the only way to keep baby happy and well.

It is a great deal of trouble; but it is a great deal more trouble to have baby sick.

The safest thing is to wash baby all over once or twice a day; and to wash it besides whenever it has had an accidental wetting. You know how easily its tender skin gets chafed.

There may be a danger in washing a child's feet and legs only. There never can be in washing it all over. Its clothes should be changed oftener than yours, because of the greater quantity baby perspires. If you clothe baby in filth, what can you expect but that it will be ill? Its clothes must never be tight, but light and warm. Baby if not properly clothed, feels sudden changes in the weather much more than you do. Baby's bedclothes must be clean oftener than yours.

Now, can you remember the things you have to mind for baby? There is—

1. Fresh air.
2. Proper warmth.
3. Cleanliness for its little body, its clothes, its bed, its room, and house.
4. Feeding it with proper food, at regular times.
5. Not startling it or shaking either its little body or its little nerves.
6. Light and cheerfulness.
7. Proper clothes in bed and up.

And management in *all* these things.

I would add one thing. It is as easy to put out a sick baby's life as it is to put out the flame of a candle. Ten minutes, delay in giving it food may make the difference.

APPENDIX III

Biographies of Florence Nightingale

The Life of Florence Nightingale, Sir E. T. Cook (2 vols., 1913).

The Life of Florence Nightingale, Sir E. T. Cook (abridged into 1 vol. by R. Nash, 1925).

Florence Nightingale, 1820–1856, I. B. O'Malley (1931).

A Lost Commander; Florence Nightingale, M. R. S. Andrews (1929).

Florence Nightingale, the wounded soldier's friend, E. Pollard (no date).

The Life of Florence Nightingale, S. Tooley (1904).

Florence Nightingale, I. C. Willis (1931).

Florence Nightingale, 1820–1910, C. Woodham-Smith (1950).

Index

Aberdeen, Lord, 25
Aberdeen, Marchioness of, 104
Aborigines, 117
À Court, Elizabeth, 25
Alexandria, 30
Army Hospital, Netley, 99
Army Hospital, Woolwich, 99
Army hospitals, mismanagement of, 39
Army Medical School, formation, 72, 73, 85
Army nurses, 40 et sqq.
Army supplies, reorganization, 49
Army transport problems, 49
Ashley, Lord, 29
Athens, 30

Baden, Grand Duchess of, 126
Balaclava, 49, 65
Barrack building, reorganization of, 84–5
Blackwell, Dr. Elizabeth, 18
Blackwood, Lady Alicia, 55
Blériot, Louis, xiii
Bonham Carter, Hilary, 3, 13, 29, 118
Bosanquet, Miss E., 135
Boulogne, 44
Bracebridge, Mr. and Mrs., 24, 26, 29, 31, 44, 65, 68, 118
Bridgeman, Mother, 65, 66
British Museum, 132
British Red Cross Society, 99

Cambridge, Duke of, 69
Christie, Miss, 4, 8
Civita Vechio, 25

Clarke, Mary, 12–13, 14, 29, 121
Clarke, Mrs., 36, 44
Clarke, Sir James, 77
Clough, Arthur Hugh, 87, 123, 124
Constantinople, 45
Craven, Mrs. Dacre, 98
Crimean War, 38 et sqq.
Cumming, Dr., 48, 62

Dawson, Sir Douglas, 136
De Redcliffe, Lord Stratford, 51
Dickens, Charles, 21, 96
District nursing, 98
Drunkenness among troops, 71
Dublin, 33
Dunant, Henri, 99–100

Edward VIIth, King, 136
Egypt, 29–30
Embley Park, 2, 13 et sqq.

Farr, Dr., 108
Feeding of hospital patients, 53
Fliedner, Mrs. Friederike, 23, 33
Fliedner, Pastor Theodor, 23, 24, 33
Florence, 1, 11
Franco-Prussian War, 99–100
Fraser's Magazine, 132
French Sisters of Charity, 30, 34
Fry, Elizabeth, 23, 43

Gale, Mrs., 9, 18
Galton, Sir Douglas, 118
'Gamp, Mrs. Sairey', 21
Gaskell, Mrs., 15–16
Gavin, Dr. Hector, 64

INDEX

Geneva, 12

Genoa, 11

Gentlewomen, Establishment for, 35–8

Good Words, 130

Grisi, 10

Hall, Dr. John, 47, 66

Health missionaries, 103–4

Herbert, Mrs. Elizabeth, 25–6, 31, 35, 40

Herbert, Sidney, 25, 26, 31, 40, 42, 51, 67, 69, 75, 82, 86–7, 108, 119

Howe, Dr., 18–20

Howe, Mrs. Julia Ward, 15

Hygiene, revolutionary ideas on, 125

Illustrated London News, 39

India, report on Army in, 129

Inkerman, Battle of, 49, 56

'Inkerman Café', 72

Institution of Kaiserswerth, The, 124

Introductory Notes on Lying-in Institutions, 130

Italy, 10

Jones, Agnes, 97

Jowett, Dr. Benjamin, 112, 115, 119, 122

Kaiserswerth, Institute of, 22, 30–2

Lablache, 10

Langston, Miss, 6

Laundry service for hospitals, 54

La Vie de Florence Rossignol, 5, 11

Lawrence, Sir John, 112

Lea Hall, 1 et sqq.

Lea Hurst, 1 et sqq.

Lees, Miss F., 99

Longfellow, Henry Wadsworth, 57

Louis Philippe, King, 12

MacDonald, Mr., 51, 52

Maison de la Providence, 34

Manning, Cardinal, 25, 26, 33, 44

Marseilles, 25, 44

Martin Chuzzlewit, 21

Matlock, 1

Maxwell, Mr. Benson, 48

McNeill, Sir John, 67, 118

Menzies, Dr. Edward, 47, 48, 51

Midwives, training of, 95

Minding Baby, 128, 142–9

Mohl, Julius, 13, 34

Mohl, Madame, 34, 118

Monckton Milnes, Richard, 27, 44

Naples, 1

Newcastle, Duke of, 48

Nice, 10

Nicholson, Marianne, 3, 13, 16–17, 118

Nicholson, Mr., 22

Nicholson, Mrs. Hannah, 22, 36

Nightingale, Florence:

Aborigines, work for, 117

Army nurses, management of, 40–1

Army supplies, reorganization, 49

Army transport problems, solving of, 49

Birth of, xiii

Burial of, 137

Childhood, 1–14

Cholera epidemic, experiences in, 37

Correspondence with nurses, 101

Death of, xiii, 137

Decline in health, 134, 136

Decorations awarded to, 100

Diaries of, 7, 11

Education of, xiii, xiv, 1–14

Eightieth birthday celebrations, 134

Events in life of, 139–41

Freedom of City awarded to, 136–7

Hygiene, revolutionary ideas of, 125

INDEX

Illness in Crimea, 68
India, report on Army in, 129
India, work for, 106–13
Journalistic tendencies of, 121–3
Letters of, 7
Notes of, 102, 103
Official opposition to, 47, 110
Opera, first visit to, 10
Order of Merit, bestowal of, 136
Paris, work in, 34
Popularity of, 68–9
Questionnaire on Indian Army, 108–9
Religious outlook of, 116–17, 131–2
Royal Commission, work on, 81–7
Soldiers, idolized by, 56, 57, 70
Statistics, interest in, 114–15
Statistical Society of England, made member of, 115
Visitors to, 101–2
Writings of, 121, 133
'Nightingale Cult', 69
Nightingale Fund, 51, 69
Nightingale School, 88, 131
Nightingale School trainees, 100–1
Nightingale, Peter, 1
Nile, River, 29
Notes on Hospitals, 88, 124, 128
Notes on Matters Affecting the British Army, 124
Notes on Nursing, 88, 124–8
Notes on Nursing for the Labouring Classes, 128, 142–9
Nurses' homes, 92
Nurses, strict training of, 92–4
Nurses' uniforms, 59

Observations, 110–11, 129
Oliver Twist, 96
Osborne, Sidney Godolphin, 51–2

Paget, Sir James, 126
Panmure, Lord, 78, 83

Paris, 44
Peel, Sir Robert, 25
Pera, 45
Pius IX, Pope, 25
Place Vendôme, 12
Porta Romana, 1
'Prig, Mrs. Betsy', 21
Prince Consort, 70
Prussia, Crown Princess of, 99

Quain's Dictionary of Medicine, 130, 131

Ragged Schools, 29
Raglan, Lord, 47, 68
Rathbone, Mr., 95–7, 98, 118
Rawlinson, Mr. R., 64
Reading room for troops, 71
Récamier, Madame, 13
Recreation centres, 72
Religious antagonisms, 60–1
Remittances to soldiers' families, 72
Riviera, The, 10
Robert Lowe, 65
Roberts, Mrs., 65, 68
Rome, 25
Romsey, 2
Royal Commission on sanitary state of India, 108
Rubini, 10
Russell, W. H., 39

Sabin, Mr., 47
Salisbury Infirmary, 28
Sanitary Commission and reforms, 65
Santa Colomba, Madre, 26
Santa Filomena, 57
Scutari, 44 et sqq.
Sellon, Miss, 43
Shore, Mary (Aunt Mai), 3, 29, 70, 71, 75, 118, 123, 124
Shore, William, 3
Sisters of Mercy, 43
Smith, Dr. Andrew, 47, 51

INDEX

Smith, Miss Frances, 2
Smith, Octavius, 7
Smith, Samuel, 3, 42
Smith, William, 2
Soldiers' wives, care of, 54-5
South Street, Mayfair, 78
Soyer, Alexis, 54, 65, 67
Soyer's Culinary Campaign, 54, 67
Spence, Dr., 48
Stanley, Miss Mary, 61-3, 65
Stewart, Mrs. Shore, 66, 98, 99
Storks, Sir Henry, 72
St. Paul's Cathedral, 5
St. Thomas's Hospital, 89-91
Suggestions for Thought, 132
Sutherland, Dr. John, 63, 64, 75, 82, 108, 118, 123

The Times, 39, 48, 51, 98
Trinitâ dei Monti, 26
Tullock, Colonel A., 67, 118

United Service Museum, 70

Vauxhall, 5
Vectis, The, 44-5
Verney, Sir Harry, 81, 118
Victoria, Queen, 9, 13, 22, 63, 70, 77-8, 125
Victorian Order of Nurses, 104
Villa Colombaia, 1
Von Bunsen, Baron, 22, 31

Wardroper, Mrs., 90, 93
Westminster Abbey, 5
Whitfield, Mr., 90
Wilberforce, William, 2
Woman Suffrage Movement, 115-16
Workhouse infirmaries reforms, 96-7
Wreford, Mr., 47